World on Fire
at the Palingenesis of Heaven & Earth

Luke McNab
Author

Gotham Books

30 N Gould St.
Ste. 20820, Sheridan, WY 82801
https://gothambooksinc.com/
Phone: 1 (307) 464-7800

Published by Gotham Books (June 3, 2022)

ISBN: 978-1-956349-74-0 (sc)
ISBN: 978-1-956349-75-7 (e)

Any people depicted in stock imagery provided by iStock are models, and such images are being used for illustrative purposes only.

Certain stock imagery © iStock.

Because of the dynamic nature of the Internet, any web addresses or links contained in this book may have changed since publication and may no longer be valid.

The views expressed in this work are solely those of the author and do not necessarily reflect the views of the publisher, and the publisher hereby disclaims any responsibility for them.

TABLE OF CONTENTS

Chapter

CHAPTER 1

INTRODUCTION

We are living in momentous times. We are the generation upon whom the ends of the world have come. Remarkable few people there are who know and realize how many prophetic scriptures have been fulfilled and are now being fulfilled in our days. The book of the prophet Daniel says: Daniel 12:4 **(KJV):**

4 "But thou, O Daniel, shut up the words, and seal the book, even to the time of the end: many shall run to and fro, and knowledge shall be increased."

Now in the time of the end we are amazed at the speed and increase of knowledge, world-wide. Never in the history of man has there been such traffic and a running to and fro, as now. The preservation of Israel as a nation; her return to the promised land, albeit in much opposition, is amazing. The revival of a language as good as dead; the victories in conflicts with nations much larger and more numerous, are something for the history books and military studies.

The words of scripture are often terse and concise, with meaning far beyond one's expectation. In the Apocalypse or Revelation, the Apostle John describes the days preceding the return of Christ, Revelation 16:17-19 (KJV)

*17 "And the seventh angel poured out his vial into the air; and there came a **great voice out of the temple of heaven,** from the throne, saying, it is done.*
*18 And there were voices, and **thunders,** and **lightnings**; and there was a **great earthquake,** such as **was not since men were upon the earth, so mighty an earthquake, and so great.***
*19 And the great city was divided into three parts, **and the cities of the nations fell**: and great **Babylon came in remembrance** before God, to give unto her the cup of the wine of the fierceness of his wrath."*

The expression, *the cities of the nations fell*, is very shocking. Imagine one city, such as New York or London. All the skyscrapers, tall buildings, towers, apartments, etc. toppling. Like a hundred nine elevens, which were 2 towers and building on the hill, what calamitous destruction and loss of life would be done! Were this instance but of an entire city, there would be fires, smoke, explosions, loss of life in the millions, gas stations aflame, gas lines ablaze, a scene not easily imagined, then imagine all the cities of the nations together, *World on Fire!*

At the return of Christ, the whole world will be on fire, the elements will melt with fervent heat, the heavens will roll back as a scroll, and a new earth and heaven will be created. From the book of Revelation billions of people will perish; in the words of Christ, no flesh would be saved, were not those days be shortened. The Apostle Peter in 2 Peter 3, compares this destruction of earth and heaven to that of Noah's Flood. This present world is reserved for fire at the Coming of Christ. The Apostle Paul likewise wrote (Acts 17:31) of this day of Judgment of those alive and dwelling on this habitable earth. Jude also describes this cataclysmic event as seen in the chapter following.

At no time in the preparation of this book, was there ever any idea of writing a critique of any book, much less that of a beloved and highly esteemed writer and professor of an evangelical seminary.

However, some differences cannot be overlooked, if one is to be faithful to the inspired, God-breathed scriptures. Of particular significance is the interpretation of the end times as seen in the third chapter of the second book of Peter; the 20th chapter of Revelations; and the book of Daniel. These differences will be dealt with in the coming chapters so just to "whet the appetite" and stir up the mind, mention is here made of two quotations from "*Things to come*," (page 553), compared with the book of the prophet Daniel. "*In this statement he seems to relate the dissolution of the present heaven and earth to the time of the judgment and perdition of ungodly men, which we know from Revelation 20:11- 15, takes place at the great white throne judgment after the millennium. There is no conclusion here. It is thus concluded that the purging (of the earth) is the act of God at the end of the millennium age after the final revolt against His authority, in which the earth, the scene of rebellion, is judged because of its curse.*"

This statement of said author is in direct contradiction to that of Daniel (2:44), speaking of the same beginning of the millennium. Daniel 2:44 (KJV):

44 " And in the days of these kings shall the God of heaven set up a kingdom, which shall never be destroyed: and the kingdom shall not be left to other people, but it shall break in pieces and consume all these kingdoms, and it shall stand forever."

Here we see that there is no purging of the earth at the end of the millennium, but rather at the beginning.

The prophet Zephaniah wrote (Zeph. 3:8*): for my determination is to gather the nations, that I may assemble the kingdoms, to pour upon them mine indignation, even my fierce anger: for all the earth shall be devoured with the fire of my jealousy."*

Again in the next verse is seen the fact that this is at the time of the renewal and restoration of the nation Israel at the end of the great tribulation and the beginning of the millennium. A similar description is given in Ezekiel 38:22,23. *"And I will plead against him with pestilence and with blood; and I will rain upon him, and upon his bands, and upon the many people that are with him, **an overflowing rain, and great hailstones, fire and brimstone**......and I will be known in the eyes of many nations, and they shall know that I am the Lord."* Yet another scripture describing the same scene is in Revelation 16:8-9. *"And the fourth angel poured out his vial upon the sun; and power was given unto him to scorch men with **fire**. And men were scorched with great heat...."* A final scripture depicting the very appearance and coming of Christ clearly describes the same scene, (2 Thessalonians 1:7-9): *"And to you who are troubled rest with us, when the Lord Jesus shall be revealed from heaven with his mighty angels, In **flaming fire**, taking vengeance on them that know not God, and obey not the Gospel of our Lord Jesus Christ: who shall be punished with **everlasting destruction** from the face of the Lord and from the glory......"*

Another erroneous point made by other famous men is found in Revelation 21:15-16 (KJV):

15 *"And he that talked with me had a golden reed to measure the city, and the gates thereof, and the wall thereof.*
16 *"And the city lieth foursquare, and the length is as large as the breadth: and he measured the city with the reed, twelve thousand furlongs. The length and the breadth and the height of it are equal."*

In the margin of some bibles and preached by many eminent men today is the statement that the city here mentioned is 1500 miles square! That is 12,000 furlongs on each side. The city has four sides, therefore the perimeter being 1,500 miles, each side would of necessity be 375 miles or 3,000 furlongs each. Quite a difference in the size of the city. One would have to call it a country!

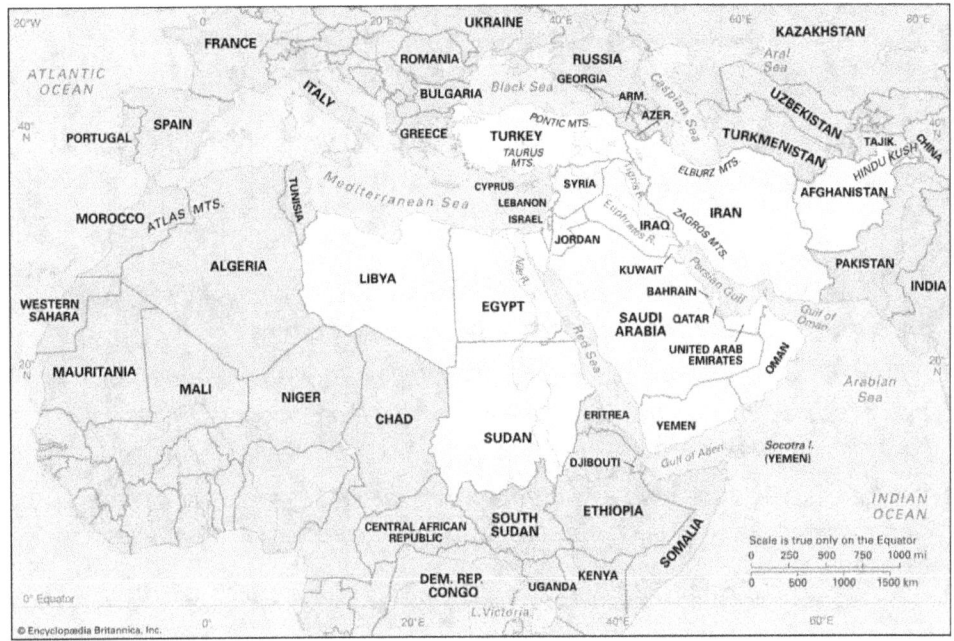

CHAPTER 2

THE PROPHETIC WORD & THE COMING OF CHRIST

This prophetic word was expressed over 2500 years ago by the prophet Haggai and explained in the book of Hebrews:(12:26-29)

26 "Whose voice then **shook the earth:** *but now he hath promised, saying,* **yet once more I shake not the earth only, but also heaven.**

27 And this word, **yet once more,** *signifieth the* **removing** *of those* **things that are shaken***, as of things that are made, that those things which cannot be shaken* **may remain.**

28 Wherefore we **receiving a kingdom** *which cannot be moved, let us have grace, whereby we may serve God acceptably with reverence and godly fear:*

29 For our God is a **consuming fire."**

In the book of Haggai it is rendered: **Haggai 2:6-7 (KJV)**

6 "For thus saith the LORD of hosts; **Yet once,** *it is a little while, and* **I will shake the heavens, and the earth, and the sea, and the dry land;**

7 And I will **shake all nations***, and the* **desire** *of all nations* **shall come***: and I will fill this house with glory, saith the LORD of hosts. "*

Not only the earth but the heavens also will be changed at this time of this world-wide earthquake at the coming of the Lord. Yet another such earthquake and shaking at the **end** of the millennium, would contradict the "*Yet once more*"of the Scriptures, so the idea of another such at that time cannot be entertained. The above passage speaks of the time of the Coming of Christ in glory and in flames of fire to execute judgment on a rebellious world. In 2 Peter, chapter 3, this is enumerated in great detail. The judgment of the Flood of Noah's time is here contrasted with this day of judgment of the living and ungodly, at the Coming of Christ in glory. This Earth, now is "*treasured up unto fire*", wrote Peter: 2 Peter 3:7

7 "But the heavens and the earth, which are now, by the same word are kept in store, **reserved unto fire against a day of judgment and perdition of ungodly men.** *"*

Note that the KJV here translates **a** *day of judgment* as **the** *day of judgment.* This is not in accordance with the original Greek. There is no definite article used in these verses in the Greek, whereas in verse 10 of Peter's passage it is used in the phrase: **The** *day of the Lord will come...* "Paul refers to this very day as **a** *day in Acts:* **17:31 (KJV)**

31 "Because he hath appointed **a day**, *in the which he will judge the world in righteousness by that man whom he hath ordained; whereof he hath given assurance unto all men, in that he hath raised him from the dead. "*

In verse 7, the word for *judgment* is the noun form of the same word used in Acts 17:31, to *judge,* (the verb form). In Greek it is krisis (κρισεως) in 2 Peter 3:7, and krino (κρινειν) in Acts 17:31. This underscores the fact that verse 7, in 2 Peter 3, refers to the time of the Coming of Christ rather than at the end of the millennium, as the results are not the same at both times, namely, judgment on the living, rather than eternal judgment of the dead in Revelation 20:11-15.

From the very context of 2 Peter 3:11-13, referring to the manner of the Coming of the Lord, the heavens on fire, rolling back with a great rushing sound, with the very elements melting and dissolving, and the works on earth burnt up, it is evident that all takes place at the very Coming of Christ. Peter notes:

11 " Seeing then that all these things shall be dissolved, **what manner of persons ought ye to be in all holy conversation and godliness,**
12 **Looking for and hasting unto the coming** *of the day of God, wherein (literally: through which) the heavens being on fire shall be dissolved, and the elements shall melt with fervent heat?*
13 Nevertheless we, according to his promise, look for new heavens and a new earth, wherein dwelleth righteousness. "

Such expectancy and manner of life could not practically be expected were these events to take place a thousand years later! At the end of the millennium! In verse 12 above the word "coming" is the Greek *parousia,* meaning *a being present, arrival, coming.* It is at the beginning or coming of this day that the heavens will be on fire and the elements melt with fervent heat, not at the end of the millennium as is thought by many.

Unfortunately, a famous Professor of theology in his signal Book, "*Things to Come",* concerning future things and the End times, on pages 552, 553, Section Seven, Chapter XXXII, 1964 edition, by Zondervan, makes some very erroneous statements; popularized by the well-known Seminary where he was a professor, and having some 215,000 copies of his book sold to date. These errors have had an adverse and detrimental effect on popular interpretations. On page 552 of his book above, he notes the correct view that claims that the judgment of 2 Peter 3:7, comes on the **living** ungodly, at the beginning of the Millennium and at the end of the 7 year period of the Great Tribulation, and not at the *end* of the Millennium, synonymous with the Great White Throne judgment of Revelation 20:11-15. On the next page 553, he mistakenly claims that both judgments occur together, at the time of the Great White throne judgment. He writes: *"It is to be noted that Peter does not say that the Day of the Lord commences with the dissolution of the present earth, but that* **within** *the day of the Lord this dissolution will take place. His word is: 'The day of the Lord will come as a thief in the night;* **in the which** *[italics mine] the heavens shall pass away with a great noise and the elements shall melt with fervent heat...' (2 Pet. 3:10). Further, Peter states: 'But the heavens and the earth, which are now, by the same word are kept in store, reserved unto Judgment and perdition of ungodly men' (2 Peter 3:7). In this statement he seems to relate the dissolution of the present heaven and earth to the time of the judgment and perdition of ungodly men, which we know from Revelation 20:11-15, takes place at the great white throne judgment after the millennium.*

There are many fallacies in these statements above by the renowned Professor with a ThD. in theology. In the first place Peter is referring to the prophecies in Isaiah 34: 1-10; and 65:17-21 (KJV):

17 " *For, behold,* **I create new heavens and a new earth**: *and the former shall not be remembered, nor come into mind.*

18 *But be ye glad and* **rejoice for ever in that which I create**: *for, behold, I create Jerusalem a rejoicing, and her people a joy.*

19 *And I will rejoice in Jerusalem, and joy in my people: and the voice of weeping shall be no more heard in her, nor the voice of crying.*

20 *There shall be no more thence an infant of days,* **nor an old man that hath not filled his days: for the child shall die a hundred years old;** *but the sinner being an* **hundred years old** *shall be accursed.*

21 *And they shall build houses, and inhabit them; and they shall plant vineyards, and eat the fruit of them.* "

Furthermore, in this prophecy, referring to the millennium age, the animal world will be at peace, as seen in verse 25:

25 " *The* **wolf and the lamb shall feed together**, *and the lion shall eat straw like the bullock: and dust shall be the serpent's meat. They shall not hurt nor destroy in all my holy mountain, saith the LORD.* "

Yet another scripture describes this time: Isaiah 11:4-9 (KJV)

4 *"But with righteousness shall he judge the poor, and reprove with equity for the meek of the earth: and* **he shall smite the earth with the rod of his mouth, and with the breath of his lips shall he slay the wicked.**

5 **And righteousness shall be the girdle of his loins, and faithfulness the girdle of his reins.**

6 **The wolf also shall dwell with the lamb, and the leopard shall lie down with the kid; and the calf and the young lion and the fatling together; and a little child shall lead them.**

7 And the cow and the bear shall feed; their young ones shall lie down together: and the lion shall eat straw like the ox.

8 And the sucking child shall play on the hole of the asp, and the weaned child shall put his hand on the cockatrice' den.

9 They shall not hurt nor destroy in all my holy mountain: for the earth shall be full of the knowledge of the LORD, as the waters cover the sea. "

Concerning this new heaven and earth which begin at the Coming of Christ and the beginning of the Day of the Lord, Isaiah writes: Isaiah 66:21-22 (KJV)

21 "And I will also take of them for priests and for Levites, saith the LORD.

*22 **For as the new heavens and the new earth**, which I will make, **shall remain before me**, saith the LORD, so shall your seed and your name remain."*

From this it is clearly seen that there is no *purging* nor *dissolution of the earth* possible at the end of the millennium, as the Professor suggests, for the new heavens and new earth will ***remain before God***, during the millennium and after Rev.20:11-15, in fact, forever. Here is a quotation from the Professor's book Page 561, Section II: *"II. THE CREATION OF THE NEW HEAVEN AND NEW EARTH*

After the dissolution of the present heaven and earth at the end of the millennium, God will create a new heaven and a new earth (Isa. 65:17, 66:22; 2 Peter 3:13; Rev. 21:1). By a definite act of creation God calls into bring a new heaven and a new earth. As God created the present heavens and earth to be the scene of His theocratic display, so God will create the new heaven and earth to be the scene of the eternal theocratic kingdom of God."

This is not in the Scriptures. No such creation is intimated between Rev.20 and Rev.21:1, as the latter verse explains (the Apostle John looking back) *"For the first heaven and the first earth **were passed away** and there was no more sea. "*Nowhere in scripture does it speak of a new heaven and earth being created again after the great white throne judgment. The above references in Isaiah 65 & 66 as well as 2 Peter 3, take place before the millennium reign of Christ. The writer referred to, mistakenly takes the Day of the Lord as being a thousand years!

The scripture does not say that but **compares** a day to God, as a thousand years and vice versa, in the sight of the Lord. The day of the Lord will also include "the day of eternity" (2 Peter 3:18), that is never ending. His whole interpretation is built on the premise that the Day of the Lord is the time of the millennium or shortly before but ending with it. Peter *does say* that the day of the Lord will *come*, or *begin*, with the passing away of the heavens with a great noise and fire and heat will burn the earth. The word *within* is an interpretation of said Professor, for *in the which,* could refer to either the day or the coming or both, as the context suggests. Paul likewise notes in 2 Thessalonians 1:8 that at the *revelation of Christ at His coming* it will be in flames of fire and the destruction of unbelievers. This judgment at the Return and Coming of Christ will be on all ungodly men, **the living** inhabitants on the earth, as writes Paul in Acts 17:31. The Greek word used here for *world,* is oikoumenen (οικουμενην), meaning *habitable world.* In Isaiah 66:15-16 (KJV), this same judgment is described saying:

15 "*For, behold, the LORD will come **with fire,** and with his chariots **like a whirlwind,** to **render his anger with fury,** and his rebuke with **flames of fire.***

*16 For by fire and by his sword will the LORD plead with **all flesh**: and the **slain of the LORD shall be many.**"*

Moreover, in Jude 14, 15, Enoch, the seventh from Adam, looking down the corridors of time, was struck, not so much by the Flood of Noah; nor by the destruction of Sodom and Gomorrah; nor the plagues of Egypt and the miraculous parting of the Red Sea; nor by the conquests of Alexander the Great; nor that of the Roman Empire; nor yet World Wars I & II, but what he prophesied about was the Lord's Coming with myriads of His saints and angels **to execute judgment** on all *the **living** ungodly* for all their hard sayings and ungodly works which ungodly men have done. Jude 1:10-16 (KJV):

10 But these speak evil of those things which they know not: but what they know naturally, as brute beasts, in those things they corrupt themselves.

11 Woe unto them! for they have gone in the way of Cain, and ran greedily after the error of Balaam for reward, and perished in the gainsaying of Core.

*12 These are spots in your feasts of charity, when they feast with you, feeding themselves without fear: clouds they are without water, carried about of winds; trees whose fruit withereth, **without fruit, twice dead, plucked up by the roots;***

*13 Raging waves of the sea, foaming out their own shame; wandering stars, **to whom is reserved the blackness of darkness for ever.***

*14 **And Enoch also,** the seventh from Adam, **prophesied of these**, saying, **Behold, the Lord cometh with ten thousands of his saints,***

*15 **To execute judgment upon all,** and to convince all that are **ungodly among them** of all their **ungodly deeds** which they have **ungodly committed**, and of all their **hard speeches** which **ungodly sinners have spoken** against him.*

*16 These **are** murmurers, complainers, **walking after** their own lusts; and **their mouth speaketh** great swelling words, having men's persons in admiration because of advantage.*

The prophet Isaiah also, as previously noted above, describes this Coming in Isaiah 34:1-4 (KJV):

*1 "**Come near, ye nations**, to hear; and hearken, ye people: **let the earth hear**, and all that is therein; the **world, and all things** that come forth of it.*

*2 For the **indignation of the LORD is upon all nations,** and **his fury upon all their armies: he hath utterly destroyed them,** he hath delivered them to the slaughter.*

*3 Their slain also shall be cast out, and their stink shall come up out of their carcases, and the **mountains shall be melted with their blood.***

*4 **And all the host of heaven shall be dissolved,** and **the heavens shall be rolled together as a scroll**: and **all their host shall fall down,** as the leaf falleth off from the vine, and as a falling fig from the fig tree."*

Isaiah is speaking here of the coming of the Lord when He returns to judge the world and set up His kingdom at the beginning of the millennium. The Apostle Peter is quoting from this very passage in 2 Peter 3:12. He uses the very Greek word *teketai* (τηκεται) = *will melt; as* in the Septuagint it is: *τακησονται* = *shall melt.* (Compare Strong's concordance #5080 Greek, verse above; Hebrew #4743 Hebrew, Isaiah 34:4). Peter writes in Greek:

12" προσδοκωντας και σπευδοντας την παρουσιαν της του θεου ημερας δι **ην ουρανοι πυρουμενοι λυθησονται** και στοιχεια

καυσουμενα **τηκεται** 13 **καινους δε ουρανους και γην καινην** κατα το επαγγελμα αυτου προσδοκωμεν εν οις δικαιοσυνη κατοικει"

12 Looking for and hasting unto the coming of the day of God, **wherein the heavens being on fire shall be dissolved**, *and the elements shall* **melt** *with fervent heat?*
13 Nevertheless we, according to his promise, **look for new heavens and a new earth,** *wherein dwelleth righteousness."*

Peter's citation is directly equivalent to Isaiah's; he is speaking of the Coming of the Lord when He will *"destroy the sinners thereof out of it",* for *"the day of the Lord is at hand; it cometh as destruction from the Almighty."* (: 6, 9). When the heavens and earth are thus destroyed there must, of necessity, be a replacement by a new heaven and new earth for which Peter says, we look, that is, at that time. Any interpretation of 2 Peter 3:10-13, as being a dissolution of heaven and earth at the end of the millennium is erroneous for that would entail a second shaking and creation of yet another third heaven and earth, which would be contrary to Hebrews 12:26,27 above. Moreover, Peter could not then logically talk about *"looking for and hastening unto the coming of the day of God,"* which would then be 1000 years away!

When *"the heavens shall be* **rolled together as a scroll***..." (verse 5),* *utterly destroying* nations (verse 2), as Isaiah describes this event, it is at the Coming of the Lord, and not at the end of His 1,000-year reign. This same event is written about in Jeremiah 25:30-32 (KJV):

*30 "Therefore prophesy thou against them all these words, and say unto them, The LORD shall **roar from on high**, and utter his voice from his holy habitation; he shall mightily roar upon his habitation; **he shall give a shout**, as they that tread the grapes, against all the inhabitants of the earth.*

*31 A noise shall come even **to the ends of the earth**; for the LORD hath a controversy with **the nations**, he will plead with all flesh; he will give them that **are wicked** to the sword, saith the LORD.*

*32 Thus saith the LORD of hosts, Behold, evil shall go forth from nation to nation, and **a great whirlwind** shall be raised up from the coasts of the earth."*

In Matthew 25:41 the nations are gathered before Christ and some are sent into the judgment of *everlasting fire.* In Rev.16:15,16, Christ comes as "*a thief in the night,*" *at* the time when the nations gather together at Armageddon. In Zephaniah the **day of the Lord comes** of the as **a day of wrath and great destruction. Zephaniah 1:14-18 (KJV):**

*14 "The **great day of the LORD is near**, it is near, and hasteth greatly, even **the voice of the day of the LORD:** the mighty man shall cry there bitterly.*

*15 That **day is a day of wrath,** a **day of trouble and distress**, a day of wasteness and desolation, **a day of darkness and gloominess, a day of clouds and thick darkness,***

16 A Day of the trumpet and alarm against the fenced cities, and against the high towers.

*17 And I will bring distress upon men, that they shall walk like blind men, **because they have sinned against the LORD:** and **their blood shall be poured out as dust,** and their flesh as the dung.*

*18 Neither their silver nor their gold shall be able to deliver them in the day of the LORD'S wrath; but the **whole land** shall be **devoured by the fire of his jealousy**: for **he shall make even a speedy riddance of all them that dwell in the land**.*

It should be noted that in this verse 18 above the Hebrew word for *Earth, (used in Genesis 1:1)* is translated as *Land.*

In Joel the day of the Lord comes with wonders in heaven and earth and such judgment as has never been seen before. Joel 3:9-17 (KJV)

*9 "Proclaim ye this among the Gentiles; **Prepare war**, wake up the mighty men, let all the men of war draw near; let them come up:*

^{10} *Beat your plowshares into swords, and your pruning hooks into spears: let the weak say, I am strong.*

^{11} *Assemble yourselves, and come, all ye heathen, and gather yourselves together round about: thither cause thy mighty ones to come down, O LORD.*

^{12} *Let the heathen be wakened, and **come up to the valley of Jehoshaphat**: for there will **I sit to judge all the heathen round about.***

^{13} *Put ye in the sickle, for the harvest is ripe: come, get you down; for the press is full, the fats overflow; for their **wickedness is great**.*

^{14} *Multitudes, multitudes in the valley of decision: **for the day of the LORD is near in the valley of decision**.*

^{15} *The **sun and the moon shall be darkened, and the stars shall withdraw their shining**.*

^{16} *The LORD also **shall roar out of Zion**, and **utter his voice from Jerusalem**; and the **heavens and the earth shall shake**: but the LORD will be the hope of his people, and the strength of the children of Israel.*

^{17} *So shall ye know that **I am the LORD your God dwelling in Zion,** my holy mountain: then shall Jerusalem be holy, and there shall no strangers pass through her any more. "*

There is every difference between the arrival, coming, and revelation of Christ and the rest of the millennial age which is one of peace and prosperity under the reign of Christ. Only at the close and end, after Satan is loosed for a time, do men rebel for the last time, gather around Jerusalem, and fire comes down from heaven, destroys them all and Satan is sent to the Lake of fire. Then comes the final judgment of the dead who will stand before Christ at the great white throne. The living, ungodly men who are alive at Christ's coming will be destroyed at the beginning and coming of Christ, as noted above, so any claim of both judgments occurring or taking place at the same time at the end is manifestly erroneous.

Unfortunately, the Professor confuses the judgment of the living, ungodly men, with the judgment of the dead in Rev. 20:11-15. Not only does Peter say that the Coming of the Day of the Lord is concomitant with the passing of the heavens with a great noise but he does **not** say it is *within* the Day of the Lord (meaning the 1,000 year period) as the Professor erroneously claims. He defines the Day of the Lord as all the millennium and hence the *within* or the phrase *in the which* then embraces this mistaken idea. Peter, on the other hand, speaks of it as the eternal day (2 Peter 3:18). The several scriptures above clearly show that Christ's Return and Coming on Mt. Olivet is also in flaming fire with the heavens and earth on fire.

All this is perfectly aligned with Peter's words in 2 Peter 3. The Scriptures do not say a thousand years is a day but as a day, in God's sight.

Another interesting point are the words that Christ speaks to the nations that come up for judgment at his coming. In Matthew 25:33-34 (KJV)

33 "And he shall set the sheep on his right hand, but the goats on the left.

*34 Then shall the King say unto them on his right hand, Come, ye blessed of my Father, **inherit the kingdom prepared for you from the foundation of the world:** "*

Apparently, these saved **inherit the new kingdom** of the **new heaven and the new earth during** the Millennium, and *this was **prepared from the foundation of the world and will last forever**,* so again no new creation of heaven and earth comes at end of the millennium, but at the beginning of it. It is also significant to note in this passage that only the **"*righteous*"** enter this kingdom. Matthew 25:44-46 (KJV)

44 "Then shall they also answer him, saying, Lord, when saw we thee an hungered, or athirst, or a stranger, or naked, or sick, or in prison, and did not minister unto thee?

45 Then shall he answer them, saying, Verily I say unto you, in as much as ye did it not to one of the least of these, ye did it not to me.

*46 And these shall go away into everlasting punishment: **but the righteous into life eternal.** "*

Likewise, a similar thought is expressed in Daniel 2:44 (KJV):

*44 " And in the days of these kings **shall the God of heaven set up a kingdom,** which shall **never be destroyed:** and the kingdom shall not be left to other people, but it shall break in pieces and consume all these kingdoms, and it shall stand for ever."*

As noted previously in Hebrews 12:28, in relation to making a new heaven and earth, it is stated:

*28 "Wherefore we **receiving a kingdom which cannot be moved**, let us have grace, whereby we may serve God acceptably with reverence and godly fear."*

There is only one kingdom and that is the millennium kingdom, into which the saved enter. There is, therefore, no new kingdom created in Revelation 21:1, but John is looking back to the beginning of it, when Christ returned in glory. Finally, in no way can it be said of Peter (as noted above by the professor) that: "*he seems to relate the dissolution of the present heaven and earth to the time of the judgment and perdition of ungodly men, which we know from Revelation 20: II-I5,*"can be correct. These are two separate events separated by approximately 1,000 years. The only relationship is that at the final great white throne judgment all will "have their day in court", so to speak; *including those* judged with death at the time of the Flood and the Coming of Christ, and too, those destroyed at the rebellion after Satan is loosed and went around deceiving mankind. It must be borne in mind also, that after the destruction by fire of those who surrounded Jerusalem, there will be no more sinners and unbelievers living on earth. It will be one "***wherein dwelleth righteousness***", to quote 2 Peter 3: 13. Pray tell, therefore, on whom would descend the judgments named in verse 7 of this same chapter, not to mention the said destruction and rolling up of the heavens and the melting of the earth! It is only "*the dead" that* are judged at the great white throne judgment, not any "living ungodly on the earth!"

A final argument proving the error of professor and several other prominent writers who place 2 Peter 3:7 and Revelation 20:11-15, as occurring at the same time, is that in 2 Peter 3:7, both the earth and the heavens are said to be "treasured up unto fire against a day of judgment and perdition of ungodly men." The day of judgment and perdition of Noah's day was some 4,400 years ago. That of Cain and others unbelievers after him and before Noah, were even before that. Others who lived ungodly after the flood, including Sodom and Gomorrah, the millions who will perish in the great tribulation, and at the coming of Christ, all have different days of "judgment and perdition". (The same Greek word is used for perish and perdition in verses 6 and 7, of 2 Peter.) Evidently these noted cannot refer to a single day or time together! They, therefore, cannot refer to the passage in 2 Peter. All these dead and ungodly will come up before Christ at the time of the second resurrection and will be judged and enter into perdition of the Lake of fire. Being dead they cannot be referred to as ungodly men, that is, as men living ungodly lives or as inhabiting the earth (Acts 17:31). Nothing in this passage of Rev. 20 intimates that heaven or earth will be burnt up at that time. They will "flee away" and "no place will be found for them" as clearly they were destroyed at the time referred to in the passage of 2 Peter 3. The Apostle John is looking back to the only "heaven and earth" he knew, that of his own day and ours today, called the first heaven and the first earth in Revelation 21:1, where he sees the new heaven and new earth, referred to by Christ as the "palingenesis" (Matthew 19:28). It is this earth and heaven that Daniel states "will stand forever" (2:44), having begun in 2 Peter 3:7, at the coming of Christ.

It is further noted that Peter in 2 Peter 3, uses exactly the same Greek word, in the noun form and verb form in verses 5, 7, 9, 17 απωλετο, απωλειας, απολεσθαι, απωλειαν, translated consecutively as: perish, perdition, perish, destruction, in the KJV. One cannot single out verse 7 and apply it to Revelation 20:11-15, when the context and usage by Peter is to different times and circumstances as in this chapter. The KJV, acknowledgely the most popular and a superb translation, in the above translation of verses 7 and 17, erred (or more precisely, put the finger on the translation balance or scale) in using the word perdition instead of destruction in verse 7, as translated in verse 17. Destruction has the connotation of a sudden, physical act, whereas perdition, from the Latin perditium, and similar French and Spanish words, means lose, that is here referring to one's eternal soul. Added to this, the Greek original in this verse 7 has it as "*a* day" not "the day of judgment and perdition of ungodly men." In conclusion, therefore, the esteemed professor and others like Dake and Scofield bible notes, incorrectly link the passages above to the same event and time, differing by about a thousand years!

Peter in this passage from verses 7-17, is actually describing the results of the actual day of the Coming of the Lord when the heavens and earth, (now stored up for fire,) according to His promise in Matthew 19:28-30, (promise referred to again in 2 Peter 3:9), actually takes place. This is what Peter yet again refers to in verse 13 as: *"But according to his promise, we look for new heavens and a new earth, in which dwelleth righteousness."*

In summary, it should be noted that the entire chapter of 2 Peter 3, is dealing with the promise of Christ found in Matthew 19:27-30, discussed in chapter 3, following. Three times this promise is here referred to by Peter; in verses 4, 9, and 13. As will be seen the promise is of a new heaven and a new earth at the return of Christ to reign on his throne of glory with the 12 Apostles likewise reigning on 12 thrones, judging the 12 tribes of Israel. Any interpretation therefore, which relegates this promise to a period after the Millennial reign, would be erroneous.

Verse 7, discusses the judgment of fire on the earth with the destruction of heaven and earth at the time of his coming. The rest of the chapter elaborates on details of that day, with no reference whatsoever to the final judgment of the great white throne judgment. It is erroneous to apply this chapter to Revelation 20:11-15, as noted previously.

CHAPTER 3

THE PALINGENESIS

It is very unfortunate that many notable preachers and writers, past and present, have embraced this erroneous idea and confused the Coming judgment on this earth and its inhabitants with the last judgment of the dead at the great white throne of Revelation 20:11-15, claiming that they are at the same time, at the end of the millennium. Another well known Bible scholar, in his excellent commentaries in his bible also makes this same error. He writes of this passage in 2 Peter 3:7, in note (i), page 223, *"Next vs. 10. This proves that the time of the renovation of the heavens and earth by fire of vs. 10-13 will be at the great white throne judgment at the end of the millennium (v.7; Rev. 20:11-15)."* This is found in the notes of both the Dake and Schofield bibles.

Peter explains in these verses above that the present heavens and earth will be destroyed by fire so we look for new heavens and new earth, according to Christ's promise. This reference to this time is found in Matthew 19:27-30 (KJV)

27 "Then answered Peter and said unto him, Behold, we have forsaken all, and followed thee; what shall we have therefore?

*28 And Jesus said unto them, Verily I say unto you, that ye which have followed me, **in the regeneration** when the **Son of man shall sit in the throne of his glory, ye also shall sit upon twelve thrones, judging the twelve tribes of Israel.***

*29 And every one that hath forsaken houses, or brethren, or sisters, or father, or mother, or wife, or children, or lands, for my name's sake, shall receive a hundredfold, and **shall inherit everlasting life**.*

30 But many that are first shall be last; and the last shall be first."

The Greek word for *regeneration* in verse 28 is παλιγγενεσια (paliggenesia), which is a combination of two Greek words, *palin* meaning *again, once more* and genesia=*genesis*. (Note that Greek γγ =gg, is pronounced as ng in English and in Greek, hence palin.) The above scripture clearly speaks of the millennial reign of Christ and the promise not only of another *genesis,* hence *"new heavens and a new earth"* but of the 12 apostles reigning on 12 thrones, judging the 12 tribes of Israel in the millennial reign of Christ.

Yet another scripture in Hebrews 12:26-28 (KJV), as quoted previously, above notes:

26 "Whose voice then shook the earth: but now he hath promised, saying, **yet once more I shake not the earth only, but also heaven.**

27 And this word, **yet once more,** *signifieth the removing of those things that are shaken, as of things that are made, that those things which cannot be shaken may remain.*

28 Wherefore **we receiving a kingdom which cannot be moved,** *let us have grace, whereby we may serve God acceptably with reverence and godly fear:"*

In Revelation 16: 18-20, there is an earthquake greater than any since man was on earth, and just preceding the coming of Christ in glory at the end of the battle of Armageddon, so it is to this phrase *"Yet once more I shake the earth,"* that reference is being made. This, therefore, would preclude another like destruction at or after the great white throne judgment! As quoted previously:

18 " And there were voices, and thunders, and lightnings; and there was a great earthquake, **such as was not since men were upon the earth,** *so mighty an earthquake, and so great.*

19 And the great city was divided into three parts, and the cities of the nations fell: and **great Babylon came in remembrance** *before God, to give unto her the cup of the wine of the fierceness of his wrath.*

20 And **every island fled away,** *and the* **mountains were not found."**

All of this occur at the end of the great tribulation at the time of Christ's return to deliver His people. Were the creation of a new heaven and new earth as of Revelation 21:1 **where there were no seas,** to occur again this movement of waters whether above or within the earth, would indeed be a contradiction of *"Yet once more I shake not the earth only, but also heaven"* of Hebrews 12:26, noted above. Therefore, it stands to reason that the new heavens and new earth begin at the Return and Coming of Christ. It is therefore concluded that in Revelation 21:1, the Apostle John is looking back to the days at the return of Christ, for at His coming the seas are raised to waters above, and on earth there is no sea, for the first heaven and the first earth (with its sea) have passed away!

The proof that John in Revelation 21:1, is looking back when he says, "*I saw a new heaven and a new earth,*" lies in the words, "*for the first heaven and the first earth **were passed away**; and there was no more sea.*" When did this occur? Previously, of course. No mention of such a stupendous event taking place, occurs in the record of scripture during the millennium or after until this announcement in Rev. 21:1. It is in 2 Peter 3:10-13, that it is related, that is, at the Coming of Christ.

The manner of how the heavens passed away is described in 2 Peter 3, and subsequent or concomitant events in the creation of this new heaven and earth, as well as the extirpation or removal of the seas on earth, now needs to be explained. First of all, it should be noted that the words of verse 5 of Revelation 21, "*Behold I make all things new,*" does not refer to this act of the creation of a new heaven and earth but to life after their creation. All things being new, refers, as the context suggests, to daily life and conditions in this new heaven and earth. All things fade, decay, grow old and perish in the present world. All things will never die, decay, grow old, or perish in the new.

The old man of 90 years will revert to his state of youth, vigor etc. when he newly turned 20 or so. Those who saw the Coming of the Lord would, at the end of the millennium, be over 1,000 years old, some about 1,050 to near 1,100 years, so they would evidently need a little "touching up!" The very tense of the verse is the present, and could perhaps be rendered, "*Behold, I am making all things new.*" In the words of the song: Never *grow old, never grow old..."*

Perhaps, as some say, God will be wiping away all tears from their eyes!

It is surely quite plausible that tears would spring up, at least at the beginning of the heavenly experience when one sees what could have been, had one done differently in this earthly life. Perhaps this is what Peter is suggesting in verse 11, "*what manner of persons ought we to be, in all holy conversation and godliness.*"

Thus, it is found in Revelation 21:2-5,

2 " And I John saw the holy city, new Jerusalem, coming down from God out of heaven, prepared as a bride adorned for her husband.

*3 And I heard a great voice out of heaven saying, **Behold, the tabernacle of God is with men**, and he will dwell with them, and they shall be his people, and God himself shall be with them, and be their God.*

*4 And God shall wipe away all tears from their eyes; and there shall be no more death, neither sorrow, nor crying, neither shall there be any more pain: for the **former things are passed away**.*

*5 And he that sat upon the throne said, **Behold, I make all things new**. And he said unto me, write: for these words are true and faithful"*

With respect to there being *no seas* on the new earth, the above passage in Revelation 16:19, where Babylon comes into remembrance before God, may give the key. In the passage is related such an earthquake, as never before seen, since man was on the earth, and the effects wherein Babylon is totally destroyed. The chapters following describe in much detail the judgment, but the significant verse is verse 21 in Revelation 18:15-22 (KJV):

15 "The merchants of these things, which were made rich by her, shall stand afar off for the fear of her torment, weeping and wailing,

16 And saying, Alas, alas, that great city, that was clothed in fine linen, and purple, and scarlet, and decked with gold, and precious stones, and

*pearls! 17 For in one hour so great riches is come to nought. **And every shipmaster, and all the company in ships, and sailors, and as many as trade by sea, stood afar off,***

18 And cried when they saw the smoke of her burning, saying, what city is like unto this great city!

*And they cast dust on their heads, and cried, weeping and wailing, saying, alas, alas, that great city, **wherein were made rich all that had ships in the sea by reason of her costliness!** for in one hour is she made desolate.*

20 Rejoice over her, thou heaven, and ye holy apostles and prophets; for God hath avenged you on her.

21 *And a mighty angel took up a stone like a great millstone, and cast it into the sea, saying, thus with violence shall that great city Babylon be thrown down, and shall be found no more at all.*

22 *And the voice of harpers, and musicians, and of pipers, and trumpeters,* **shall be heard no more at all in thee; and no craftsman, of whatsoever craft he be, shall be found any more in thee; and the sound of a millstone shall be heard no more at all in thee; "**

Verse 21 speaks of a mighty angel who took a stone, like a great millstone, and cast it into the sea, depicting how Babylon would be found no more at all. This is very significant especially when compared with verse 17 above, "**And every shipmaster, and all the company in ships, and sailors, and as many as trade by sea, stood afar off,** *and cried when they saw the smoke of her burning, saying, what city is like unto this great city."* Verses 23-24 complete the picture:

23 *And the light of a candle* **shall shine no more at all in thee;** *and the voice of the bridegroom and of the bride shall be heard no more at all in thee: for thy merchants were the great men of the earth; for by thy sorceries were all nations deceived.*

24 *And in her was found the blood of prophets, and of saints, and of all that were slain upon the earth.*

Here the total destruction and annihilation of Babylon is described. Her **empire on the seas** is totally blotted out. This is really accomplished by the mighty angel who threw a great millstone into the sea. Not only Babylon, but also the sea was obliterated! In other words, in the words of the prophet Habakkuk, **3:10 ,**

10 *"The mountains saw thee, and they trembled: the overflowing of the water passed by:* **the deep uttered his voice, and lifted up his hands on high. "**

As will be seen in the following chapter, this represents the result of the creation of the new heaven and new earth when the waters of the deep are raised above the earth to the heavens as in Genesis, forming and providing now, an eternal protecting shield for the earth.

All of these accord with 2 Peter 3:10-13, in the destruction of the earth by fire; the melting of the elements; and the formation of the new heavens with the waters above. The representation of Babylon as the hub of disobedient, ungodly men, forming their own city, economy, industry, entertainment and idolatrous religion, are all represented in Babylon the great, a true offspring of the original disobedient Babel and Babylon of Genesis which wanted to go its own way contrary to the will and plan of God. The amalgamation of all the elements found in Revelation 16, enables the conception of this new heaven and new earth where there is no more sea.

In Revelation 18:21 the analogy between the destruction of Babylon and the strong angel that threw a great millstone into the sea with attendant noise and splash is significant. In Habakkuk (3:10) the sea roars and lifts its form on high (waters above, no more sea) and this would cause the continental plates to flow back, levelling the mountains, filling the valleys as seen in Isaiah 40. By this action Babylon with her sailors, sea captains, ships, navies, maritime emporiums including grain, animals, industrial material, all manner of merchandise, ship builders' enterprises, etc. are totally obliterated. This causes grief, inconsolably weeping and mourning as seen in Revelation 18:21-24 (KJV) and quoted previously:

21 *"And a mighty angel took up a stone like a great millstone, and cast it into the sea, saying, thus with violence shall that **great city Babylon be thrown down, and shall be found no more at all.***

22 *And the voice of harpers, and musicians, and of pipers, and trumpeters, shall be heard no more at all in thee; and **no craftsman, of whatsoever craft he be**, shall be found any more in thee; and the sound of a millstone shall be heard no more at all in thee;*

23 *And the light of a candle shall shine no more at all in thee; and the voice of the bridegroom and of the bride shall be heard no more at all in thee: for thy **merchants were the great men of the earth**; for by thy sorceries were all nations deceived.*

24 And in her was found the blood of prophets, and of saints, and of all that were slain upon the earth. "

In this same chapter the maritime emporiums are fatally affected. Revelation 18:9-19 (KJV)

9 "And they who have committed fornication and lived deliciously with her, shall bewail her, and lament for her, when they shall see the smoke of her burning,

*10 Standing afar off for the fear of her torment, saying, Alas, alas, **that great city Babylon, that mighty city! for in one hour is thy judgment come.***

*11 **And the merchants of the earth shall weep and mourn over her; for no man buyeth their merchandise any more:***

*12 The **merchandise of gold, and silver, and precious stones**, and of pearls, and fine linen, and purple, and silk, and scarlet, and all thyine wood, and all manner vessels of ivory, and all manner vessels of most precious wood, and of brass, and iron, and marble,*

*13 And cinnamon, and odours, and ointments, and frankincense, and wine, and oil, and **fine flour, and wheat, and beasts, and sheep, and horses**, and chariots, and slaves, and souls of men.*

14 And the fruits that thy soul lusted after are departed from thee, and all things which were dainty and goodly are departed from thee, and thou shalt find them no more at all.

15 The merchants of these things, which were made rich by her, shall stand afar off for the fear of her torment, weeping and wailing,

16 And saying, Alas, alas, that great city, that was clothed in fine linen, and purple, and scarlet, and decked with gold, and precious stones, and pearls!

*17 For in one hour so great riches is come to nought. **And every shipmaster, and all the company in ships, and sailors, and as many as trade by sea, stood afar off,***

*18 **And cried when they saw the smoke of her burning, saying,** what city is like unto this great city!*

*19 **And they cast dust on their heads, and cried, weeping and wailing, saying, Alas, alas, that great city,** wherein were made rich all that had ships in the sea by reason of her costliness! for in one hour is she made desolate. "*

It is important to note that all these judgments are connected in Revelation 16, with the coming of Christ at the end of the battle of Armageddon. The sequence of these judgments as noted in **2 Peter 3:7-13**, could be concurrent or following each other with the result of a new heaven, a new earth, and no more seas!

In the book of Revelation, the chapters do not necessarily follow in a strict chronological manner. There are intercalary chapters where one chapter may give a view of what is happening or has happened in heaven, then a following one brings one up to speed, so to speak, of what is or has happened on earth. For example, in Revelation 16 is given a reference to Babylon the great coming into judgment at time of the great earthquake, then the following chapters give details of this event from an earthly viewpoint and also of what is occurring in heaven.

CHAPTER 4

HABAKKUK'S VISION

The book of the prophet Habakkuk, though seldom preached on, sheds very significant light on the Coming Day of the Lord. In three brief chapters he describes wonders to come, focusing on the revelation of the Lord in the final deliverance of His people. He writes: Habakkuk 1:5 (KJV)

5 "*Behold ye among the heathen, and regard, and wonder marvellously: for I will work a work in your days, which ye will not believe, though it be told you.*"

As to the time of the fulfillment of his prophecies he notes: Habakkuk 2:2-3 (KJV)

2 "*And the LORD answered me, and said, Write the vision, and make it plain upon tables, that he may run that readeth it.*
3 **For the vision is yet for an appointed time, but at the end it shall speak,** *and not lie:* **though it tarry, wait for it;** *because it will surely come, it will not tarry.*"

The time of the execution of this vision is at the end time when God comes to deliver His people; he chastens the nations; the sun and moon stand still in consternation; the depths of the sea are moved and utters its deep voice and **raises itself visibly on high!** This may well be a repeat of Genesis (1:8) when the waters of the deep were divided and parted forming the heavens, (Hebrew "Hashamim"= waters above), and the sea below. All these details may substantiate Peter's description of "new heavens and new earth". The explanation is found in Habakkuk 3:3-19 (KJV):

3 "God came from **Teman,** and the Holy One from mount **Paran**. Selah. His **glory covered the heavens,** and the earth was full of his praise.

4 And his brightness was as the light; he had horns coming out of his hand: and there was the hiding of his power.

5 Before him went the pestilence, **and burning coals went forth at his feet.**

6 He stood, and measured the earth: **he beheld, and drove asunder the nations**; and the **everlasting mountains were scattered**, the **perpetual hills did bow**: his ways are everlasting.

7 I saw the tents of Cushan in affliction: and the curtains of the land of Midian did tremble.

8 Was the LORD displeased against the rivers? was thine anger against the rivers? **was thy wrath against the sea,** that thou didst ride upon thine horses and thy chariots of salvation?

9 Thy bow was made quite naked, according to the oaths of the tribes, even thy word. Selah. Thou didst cleave the earth with rivers.

10 **The mountains saw thee,** and they trembled: **the overflowing of the water passed by: the deep uttered his voice, and lifted up his hands on high.**

11 **The sun and moon stood still in their habitation:** at the light of thine arrows they went, and at the shining of thy **glittering spear.**

12 Thou didst march through the land in **indignation**, thou didst **thresh the heathen** in anger.

13 Thou wentest forth **for the salvation of thy people, even for salvation with thine anointed**; thou woundedst the head out of the house of the wicked, by discovering the foundation unto the neck. Selah.

14 Thou didst strike through with his staves the head of his villages: they came out as a whirlwind to scatter me: their rejoicing was as to devour the poor secretly.

15 Thou didst walk through the sea with thine horses, through the heap of great waters.

16 **When I heard, my belly trembled; my lips quivered at the voice: rottenness entered into my bones, and I trembled in myself, that I might rest in the day of trouble:** when he cometh up unto the people, he will invade them with his troops.

17 Although the fig tree shall not blossom, neither shall fruit be in the vines; the labour of the olive shall fail, and the fields shall yield no meat; the flock shall be cut off from the fold, and there shall be no herd in the stalls:

18 Yet I will rejoice in the LORD, I will joy in the God of my salvation.

19 The LORD God is my strength, and he will make my feet like hinds' feet, and he will make me to walk upon my high places. To the chief singer on my stringed instruments."

In verse 10 above the prophet is describing the action of the sea. The KJV translates *hands* but the Hebrew sense and Septuagint Greek are even more explicit, meaning that the sea lifted up its waves and **form** on high, making it visible to all! Hebrew:

יראוך יחילו הרים זרם מים עבר **נתן תהום קולו רום ידיהו נשא:**

The Greek Septuagint has it: εδωκεν η αβυσσος φωνην αυτης, υψος **φαντασιας αυτης**. *The deep uttered her voice and raised the height of her form on high.* Here both the Hebrew words and the Greek *fantasias* convey the idea of showing oneself, and making known one's form.

It is conceivable that the **lifting up of the sea** could come about because the elements melt with fervent heat and so hydrogen and oxygen would then rise up on high! This is of course an attempt to reconcile science with what is in effect the absolutely unsearchable power and majesty of God who spoke and the world came into being. 2 Peter *3*:10-13 would then be explained more clearly.

The significance of this movement of waters to the heavens lies in the fact that this would cause such an earthquake as noted in Revelation 16:18, as the pressure now being exerted on the plates of the seas between continents would be lifted and naturally the continental plates would flow back together! Thus, Brazil would again fit into the western part of Africa, the rocky mountains would flow back eastward and there would not be found any isles. After the Flood, in the time of Peleg, the weight of the waters from above from the Flood, caused the continental plates to shift thus forming the rocky mountains, the Andes, the Alps, and Himalayas, etc. (The Himalayas being over 5 miles high, [8,848 meters], would not have been that high at the time of the Flood which rose 15 feet above the highest mountain! Were the mountains that high before the Flood, it would necessitate over 5 miles depth of water to cover all the earth!) This is the true meaning of the scripture that in Peleg's day *"the earth was divided."* Peleg means *division.* That was not the division of the nations at Babel, which was earlier in the days of the sons of Japhet:

*5" By these were the isles of the Gentiles divided in their lands; every one after his
tongue, after their families, in their nations."*

Genesis 10:5(KJV)

*5" And unto Eber were born two sons: the name of one was Peleg; for in
his days was **the earth** divided; and his brother's name was Joktan."*

The crowning argument for the new heavens of 2 Peter 3:10-13, lies
perhaps, in the words of Isaiah, previously quoted: (65:17-20 KJV)

17 "For, behold, **I create new heavens and a new earth**: and the
former shall not be remembered, nor come into mind.

18 But be ye glad and rejoice for ever in that which I create: for, behold, I
create Jerusalem a rejoicing, and her people a joy.

19 And I will rejoice in Jerusalem, and joy in my people: and **the
voice of weeping shall be no more heard in her, nor the voice
of crying**.

20 There shall be no more thence an infant of days, nor an old man that hath
not filled his days: for the **child shall die** an hundred years old; but the
sinner being an hundred years old shall be accursed."

It can therefore be concluded that in the millennium there will be new
heavens and new earth; there will be some death, but generally all will live out
lives, evidently to 1,000 years; childbirth will be easier, and not sorrowful. Clearly,
the first heaven and first earth of Revelation 21:1, would also refer to that time
before the millennium, that is to say, the day of the Apostle John and up to our
day, and not that of the new heavens and earth of the millennium. The very
nature of animals will be changed as seen in Isaiah 65:22-25 (KJV)

22 *"They shall not build, and another inhabit; they shall not plant, and
another eat: for as the days of a tree are the days of my people, and mine
elect shall long enjoy the work of their hands.*

*23 They shall not labour in vain, nor **bring forth for trouble; for they are the seed of the blessed of the LORD, and their offspring with them.***

24 And it shall come to pass, that before they call, I will answer; and while they are yet speaking, I will hear.

*25 **The wolf and the lamb shall feed together**, and the lion shall eat straw like the bullock: and dust shall be the serpent's meat. **They shall not hurt nor destroy in all my holy mountain, saith the LORD. "***

All this accords with the Scripture of Romans 8:19-23 (KJV)

*19 "For the earnest expectation of the creature waiteth for the **manifestation of the sons of God**.*

20 For the creature was made subject to vanity, not willingly, but by reason of him who hath subjected the same in hope,

*21 Because the **creature itself also shall be delivered from the bondage of corruption** into the glorious liberty of the children of God.*

22 For we know that the whole creation groaneth and travaileth in pain together until now.

*23 And not only they, but ourselves also, which have the firstfruits of the Spirit, even we ourselves groan within ourselves, **waiting for the adoption, to wit, the redemption of our body. "***

This new heaven and earth, with the waters of the deep now above, seem to accord with Revelation 21, *"and there was no more sea. "* As noted above, the continental plates would shift back with the great earthquake of Revelation 16:18. The result would be exactly as prophesied in Isaiah 40:3-5 (KJV)

3 The voice of him that crieth in the wilderness, Prepare ye the way of the LORD, make straight in the desert a highway for our God.

*4 **Every valley shall be exalted, and every mountain and hill shall be made low**: and the crooked shall be made straight, and the rough places plain:*

5 And the glory of the LORD shall be revealed, and all flesh shall see it together: for the mouth of the LORD hath spoken it.

CHAPTER 5

THE RUSSIAN CONNECTION

The description of the invasion of Israel has long been foretold by the prophets. In Ezekiel chapters 38, 39, a detailed account is given. Modern scholars are at some variance as to the time of it, though it is at the end times as noted in Ezekiel 38:8-12 (KJV):

8 "After many days thou shalt be visited: **in the latter years thou shalt come into the land** *that is brought back from the sword, and is* **gathered out of many people, against the mountains of Israel,** *which have been always waste: but it is brought forth out of the nations, and they shall dwell safely all of them.*

9 **Thou shalt ascend and come like a storm, thou shalt be like a cloud to cover the land, thou, and all thy bands, and many people with thee.**

10 Thus saith the Lord GOD; It shall also come to pass, that at the same time shall things come into thy mind, and thou shalt think an evil thought:

11 And thou shalt say, I will go up to the land of unwalled villages; I will go to them that are at rest, that dwell safely, all of them dwelling without walls, and having neither bars nor gates,

12 To take a spoil, and to take a prey; **to turn thine hand upon the desolate places that are now inhabited, and upon the people that are gathered out of the nations, which** *have gotten cattle and goods, that dwell in the midst of the land. "*It will be shown from the Scriptures, contrary to many current interpretations, that the Russian invasion, noted above, takes place before the Day of the Lord and His Coming to deliver His people at the end of the battle of Armageddon. It does not take place before the Tribulation; at its beginning; nor in mid tribulation, as is frequently taught. The proof of these statements can be found by comparing scripture with scripture, here particularly, between the prophecies in chapters of Joel 1-3; Ezekiel 38, 39; and Revelation 16-19. As the scripture says, in the paronomasia of the Hebrew,

צו לצו צו לצו קו לקו קו לקו קו לקו זעיר (tsav lasav tsav lasav kav lakav kav lakav zeir sham zeir sham) and the palindrome of English, in Isaiah 28:10 (KJV):

10" *For precept must be upon precept, precept upon precept; line upon line, line upon line; here a little, and there a little: "*

In short, expect repetition, especially of important and necessary topics. It should be noted that Joel 2:2, clearly states that the invasion of the *northern* army is on such a scale as has never happened before nor will take place again for many generations to come. (Perhaps the many generations could refer to the final rebellion after Satan is loosed at the end of the millennium and a vast number from all nations, as the sands of the sea, assemble around Jerusalem and fire falls from heaven destroying them all.) In Joel 2:1-2 (KJV):

1" *Blow ye the trumpet in Zion, and sound an alarm in my holy mountain: let all the inhabitants of the land tremble:* **for the day of the LORD cometh, for it is nigh at hand;**
2 **A day of darkness and of gloominess, a day of clouds and of thick darkness,** *as the morning spread upon the mountains:* **a great people and a strong; there hath not been ever the like, neither shall be any more after it, even to the years of many generations."**

This nation is identified in verse 20, as *the northern army.* It can only be Russia and her cohorts as identified and described in Ezekiel 39:1-2,

1 *"Therefore, thou son of man, prophesy against Gog, and say, Thus saith the Lord GOD; Behold, I am against thee, O Gog, the chief prince of Meshech and Tubal:*
2 *And I will turn thee back, and leave but the sixth part of thee, and will cause thee* **to come up from the north parts***, and will bring thee upon the mountains of Israel: "*

In the original Hebrew, translated in the KJV as, **from the north parts,** are the words *miyarketi tsaphon,* signifying *from the extremities of the north,* as seen in the Hebrew phrase below, in the KJV, "from the north parts, and will bring them upon the mountains of Israel."

מירכתי **צפון** והבאותך על־הרי ישראל:

This northern army is destroyed on the mountains of Israel, between the Dead sea and the Mediterranean sea, by divine intervention including great hail stones, overflowing rain, brimstone and pestilence. That Ezekiel 39:11 and Joel 2:20 are speaking of the very same event at the approach of the Day of the Lord, there can be no doubt, with a comparison of both scriptures. Ezekiel 39:11 (KJV)

*11 "And it shall come to pass in that day, that I will give unto Gog a **place there of graves in Israel, the valley of the passengers on the east of the sea: and it shall stop the noses of the passengers**: and there shall they bury Gog and all his multitude: and they shall call it The Valley of Hamongog."*
Joel 2:20-21 (KJV)

*20 "But I will remove far off from you the northern army, and will drive him into a land barren and desolate, **with his face toward the east sea, and his hinder part toward the utmost sea**, and **his stink shall come up, and his ill savour shall come up,** because he hath done great things.*
21 Fear not, O land; be glad and rejoice: for the LORD will do great things."

Note that the location in both passages is identical. The detail that Gog and company have their face toward the Dead sea and their back toward the Mediterranean sea is very significant; it is describing a great army in **full flight!** The appearance of the Lord in the Day of the Lord is at hand as described in the previous chapter of Joel. Moreover, in Habakkuk chapter 3, and Isaiah 34, Christ's return is from the S.E of Israel, going towards the mount of Olives. It is clear too, that the army is fleeing from utmost catastrophes of nature, as stated in Ezekiel 38:18-23 (KJV)

18 " And it shall come to pass at the same time when Gog shall come against the land of Israel, saith the Lord GOD, that my fury shall come up in my face.

*19 For in my jealousy and **in the fire of my wrath have I spoken**, Surely in that day **there shall be a great shaking in the land of Israel;***

*20 So that the fishes of the sea, and the fowls of the heaven, and the beasts of the field, and all creeping things that creep upon the earth, and all the men that are upon the face of **the earth, shall shake at my presence, and the mountains shall be thrown down**, and the steep places shall fall, and every wall shall fall to the ground.*

21 And I will call for a sword against him throughout all my mountains, saith the Lord GOD: every man's sword shall be against his brother.

*22 And **I will plead against him with pestilence and with blood**; and **I will rain upon him, and upon his bands, and upon the many people that are with him, an overflowing rain, and great hailstones, fire, and brimstone.***

23 Thus will I magnify myself, and sanctify myself; and I will be known in the eyes of many nations, and they shall know that I am the LORD."

Fire, brimstone, hail the size of a 50 lbs. talent, will cause the army to flee to the mountains and desert from fear of the Lord. The Army is doubtless seeking refuge from the talent size hailstones and overflowing rain, as they flee to the hills of the numerous caves of Quamran and the limestone cliffs above, and in the mountains and deserts of Israel, between the Dead Sea and the Mediterranean Sea. The accuracy of the description of these hailstones, plagues and upheavals of nature is confirmed in Revelation 16:8-11 (KJV):

*8 " And the fourth angel poured out his vial upon the sun; and power was given unto him **to scorch men with fire.***

*9 And men were scorched with great heat, and blasphemed the name of God, which hath power over **these plagues:** and they repented not to give him glory.*

*10 And the fifth angel poured out his vial upon the seat of the beast; and his **kingdom was full of darkness**; and they gnawed their tongues for pain,*

11 And blasphemed the God of heaven because of their pains and their sores, and repented not of their deeds."

The great hail is noted in verse 21 of the same chapter in Revelation 16:21 (KJV):

*21 " **And there fell upon men a great hail out of heaven, every stone about the weight of a talent**: and men blasphemed God because of **the plague of the hail**; for the plague thereof was exceeding great."*

Yet another significant comparison and occurrence is the invitation to the fowls of the air to feast on the flesh of these defeated armies.

Revelation 19:16-19 (KJV)

16 "And he hath on his vesture and on his thigh a name written, KING OF KINGS, AND LORD OF LORDS.

*17 And **I saw an angel standing in the sun; and he cried with a loud voice, saying to all the fowls that fly in the midst of heaven, Come and gather yourselves together unto the supper of the great God;***

*18 **That ye may eat the flesh of kings, and the flesh of captains, and the flesh of mighty men, and the flesh of horses, and of them that sit on them, and the flesh of all men, both free and bond, both small and great.***

19 And I saw the beast, and the kings of the earth, and their armies, gathered together to make war against him that sat on the horse, and against his army."

Together with this scripture is that of Ezekiel 39:3-6 (KJV)

3 "And I will smite thy bow out of thy left hand, and will cause thine arrows to fall out of thy right hand.

*4 **Thou shalt fall upon the mountains of Israel, thou, and all thy bands, and the people that is with thee: I will give thee unto the ravenous birds of every sort, and to the beasts of the field to be devoured.***

*5 **Thou shalt fall upon the open field:** for I have spoken it, saith the Lord GOD.*

6 And I will send a fire on Magog, and among them that dwell carelessly in the isles: and they shall know that I am the LORD."

There can be no doubt that the references in Ezekiel 38, 39, refer to the same events which occur at the time of the battle of Armageddon and at the approach of the day of the Lord, His coming and **Presence**, as seen in Joel 2:10-11 :

10 " The earth shall quake before them; the heavens shall tremble: the sun and the moon shall be dark, and the stars shall withdraw their shining:
11 ***And the LORD shall utter his voice before his army****: for his camp is very great: for he is strong that executeth his word:* **for the day of the LORD is great and very terrible; and who can abide it? "**

This verse ties in with Ezekiel 38:20 quoted above where the Presence of the Lord and subsequent destruction of the northern army are described, all on the Day of the Lord.

As some confusion has been caused by many expositors in the use of Biblical terminology, it may be well to clarify how names of people and places are identified in the scriptures. The scriptures never use the same name to describe two different entities, and there is consistency throughout the scripture in identifying names, persons, and places. In the book of Daniel, for example, the term, "*the king of the north,*" *is* used to describe the king of the northern kingdom of Seleucia or of the Seleucid dynasty, formed by Seleucus Nicator, who, at Alexander's death, took over Mesopotamia, Levant, Persia, part of India. Cassandra, controlled Macedonia and Greece. Lysimachus controlled Thrace and Asia minor. The northern kingdom of the four kingdoms into which the empire of Alexander the Great was divided after his death, is the one referred to in Daniel as the King of the North. The Southern kingdom under Ptolemy I, (Soter) formed the Ptolemaic Dynasty of Egypt and is referred to as the King of the South.

The King of the North in Scripture only refers to this northern country. He is sometimes referred to as the Assyrian and Rome took over this area making Seleucid on the Tigris the capital. That this King of the North is the Antichrist, appears from Daniel 11:36-44 (KJV)

*36 "And the king shall do according to his will; and **he shall exalt himself, and magnify himself above every god, and shall speak marvellous things against the God of gods, and shall prosper till the indignation be accomplished: for that is determined shall be done.***

*37 Neither shall he regard the God of his fathers, nor the desire of women, nor regard any god: **for he shall magnify himself above all.***

38 But in his estate shall he honour the God of forces: and a god whom his fathers knew not shall he honour with gold, and silver, and with precious stones, and pleasant things.

39 Thus shall he do in the most strong holds with a strange god, whom he shall acknowledge and increase with glory: and he shall cause them to rule over many, and shall divide the land for gain.

*40 And **at the time of the end shall the king of the south push at him: and the king of the north shall come against him like a whirlwind**, with chariots, and with horsemen, **and with many ships**; and he shall enter into the countries, and shall overflow and pass over.*

*41 He shall enter also into the glorious land, and many countries shall be overthrown: but these shall escape out of his hand, even **Edom,** and **Moab,** and the chief of the children of **Ammon.***

42 He shall stretch forth his hand also upon the countries: and the land of Egypt shall not escape.

43 But he shall have power over the treasures of gold and of silver, and over all the precious things of Egypt: and the Libyans and the Ethiopians shall be at his steps.

*44 **But tidings out of the east and out of the north** shall trouble him: therefore, he **shall go forth with great fury to destroy,** and utterly to make away many. "*

Tidings out of the North refer to Russia coming down to Israel, and all the Kings of the East as noted in Revelation 16:13-16 (KJV)

13 "And I saw three unclean spirits like frogs come out of the mouth of the dragon, and out of the mouth of the beast, and out of the mouth of the false prophet.

*14 For they are **the spirits of devils, working miracles, which go forth** unto the **kings of the earth** and of the whole world, **to gather them to the battle of that great day of God Almighty.***

*15 Behold, I **come as a thief.** Blessed is he that watcheth, and keepeth his garments, lest he walk naked, and they see his shame.*

^{16} *And **he gathered them together into a place called** in the Hebrew tongue **Armageddon**."*

Many expositors, including those previously referred to, confound this King of the North, the Assyrian, whom only Daniel calls by this name, with the Russian Armies, as seen on pages 355, 356, of previously cited book: *"The invasion of Palestine by the northern confederacy will bring the Beast and his armies to the defense of Israel as her protector. This invasion is described by Daniel: (Dan 11:40b-45). It is difficult to determine the activities of the nations involved in this chapter. Many have felt that the above invasion records that of the King of the South. However, in verse 36 the 'wilful king' previously identified as the Beast, is introduced to us and his activities seem to be outlined in what follows. Verses 40- 45 can hardly describe the activities of the combined forces of the Kings of the North and the South, for the pronoun 'they' would have been used. Since 'he' is used, the passage must describe further the activities of the Wilful King."*

Nowhere in the context of the invasion of Israel, can be found this term *"Kings of the North"* used, except in Jeremiah 25:26, where all nations are mentioned as drinking of the wine of God's wrath. It is used normally in the singular, *"King of the North"* and that only in the book of Daniel. The King of the North is never allied with the Russian group, so no wonder confusion is experienced with the above interpretation! On the other hand, it is not surprising that in verse 41 of Daniel chapter 11 above, that Moab (south east of Israel and part of Saudi Arabia) and the children of Ammon, (the modern Jordanians, Amman being their capital) escape, as they are even today allied in purposes and affiliation, with Iraq, the area from which the King of the North comes. Every scripture falls into place when rightly compared the one with the other. The pages 355, 356, referred to above, as well as the following page 357, are rife with suppositions about the northern confederacy uniting with the Beast, which have no scriptural foundation whatsoever.

Another ally of the Russian group is Gomer, a son of Japhet the elder, one of the three sons of Noah. This is clearly conceded and agreed to be Germany. On the other hand the above cited Professor and the Seminary are in error to say that Togarmah, one of the three sons of Gomer, is modern day Turkey and/or Armenia. The prophet Ezekiel refers to him in these words in Ezekiel 38:5- 6 (KJV)

5 "Persia, Ethiopia, and Libya with them; all of them with shield and helmet:

*6 Gomer, and all his bands; **the house of Togarmah of the north quarters**, and all his bands: and many people with thee."*

As expressed previously the Hebrew translated here as **north quarters** means *"recesses or extremities of the north,"* therefore could not apply to Turkey. However, Togarmah or Thorgama, as the Greeks have it, clearly expresses the connection of the Scandinavian god Thor with the name of these people. From their location and history we know that both Norway and Sweden come from Germanic tribes descended from Gomer. The location of significant portions of their land within the Arctic circle, leaves no possibility of error as to their identification in this portion of scripture.

In saying this, however, one is not denying the real probability that either or both Turkey or Armenia could belong to this northern confederacy. Page 339 of the same book quoted above is somewhat at variance with this passage of Scripture.

The Hebrew words for the **north quarters,** is translated **sides if the north** as seen in Isaiah 14:13 (KJV):

*13 "For thou hast said in thine heart, I will ascend into heaven, I will exalt my throne above the stars of God: I will sit also upon the mount of the congregation, **in the sides of the north**:"*

God replies in Isaiah 14:15-16 (KJV)

*15 Yet thou shalt be brought down to hell, **to the sides of the pit.***

16 They that see thee shall narrowly look upon thee, and consider thee, saying, Is this the man that made the earth to tremble, that did shake kingdoms;

The meaning therefore is the **recesses or sides** of the pit, that is the **uttermost extremities or recesses.** A comment on the verse in Ezekiel 38:8, *"they shall dwell safely all of them"* and 1 Thessalonians 5:2-3 (KJV):

2 "For yourselves know perfectly that the day of the Lord so cometh as a thief in the night.

*3 For when **they shall say,** Peace and safety; then sudden destruction cometh upon them, as travail upon a woman with child; and they shall not escape. "*

Some argue that Israel is not at peace during the Great Tribulation, so this invasion cannot be at that time. It should be noted that it does not say Israel is saying this or being described as at peace, but rather the expression is *"**they shall say"*** evidently referring to the world in general. Antichrist will have conquered Egypt and Africa and secured the vital Oil route as explained in the coming chapter, so all say peace and safety and Christ comes "as a thief in the night" and finds all unprepared, as seen too in **Revelation 16:15-16 (KJV)**

15 "Behold, I come as a thief. Blessed is he that watcheth, and keepeth his garments, lest he walk naked, and they see his shame.

16 And he gathered them together into a place called in the Hebrew tongue Armageddon."

Similarly, this coming of the Lord, *"as a thief in the night"* in 2 Peter 3:10 and 1 Thessalonians 5:4, above expresses the unpreparedness and unexpected nature of His Coming.

In page 230 of *"Things to come"* the noted professor again misinterprets the above verse in 2 Peter 3:10, writing, *"2 Peter 3:10 gives authority for including the entire millennium age within this period. If the day of the Lord did not begin until the second advent, since that event is preceded by signs, the Day of the Lord could not come as a 'thief in the night,' unexpected and unheralded, as it is said it will come in 1 Thessalonians 5:2."*

Nowhere does the idea of being "*unheralded*" with respect to "Coming as a thief" expressed as no thief ever heralds his coming! So, on page 231, the next page of his book, serious and erroneous conclusions, as noted below, are reached by that author. He writes: *"It is thus concluded that the Day of the Lord is that extended period of time beginning with God's dealing with Israel after the rapture at the beginning of the tribulation period and extending through the second advent and the millennium age unto the creation of the new heavens and new earth after the millennium."* Yet again, *"Further it will include all the events of the millennium age, with the final revolt of Satan (Rev. 20:7-10); the great white throne judgment (Rev.20:11-15); and the purging of the earth (2 Peter 3:10-13).* "All of these conclusions are manifestly contrary to the scripture as already shown.

Not only is the expression "Behold I come as a thief " repeated in Revelation 16:15, at the time of the gathering of the nations at Armageddon, just before this coming of Christ, but the verse explains that the context deals with watchfulness and unpreparedness which causes one to be found naked and ashamed because one is not watchful, but undressed, and probably sleeping! The simile has nothing at all to do with being "unheralded" as no thief as stated ever heralds his coming. There are many signs and warnings of the coming of this day throughout scripture, but this facet of Christ's coming as a thief is not applicable in this context. To use this as an argument to extend the day of the coming and return of the Lord to a thousand years, as the writer claims on page 230, 231 of his books "Things to come" is therefore fallacious.

CHAPTER 6

THE ANTICHRIST & THE ARABS

The Babylonian King Nebuchadnezzar II, about 605-562 B.C. had a dream in which was given to him a revelation of how his Empire would fare in succeeding years, until subsequently and finally replaced and destroyed by God's eternal kingdom. He had been thinking about this on his bed. Being much troubled about it he called in his soothsayers, magicians, astrologers and chief men of his empire and asked for an interpretation. He could not remember the dream and demanded, under penalty of death, that they tell him both the dream and the interpretation. Naturally no one could do so, and the young Hebrew captive Daniel, being himself in danger, was called in. Asking for a brief respite, Daniel and his three other young captives prayed and received the historically correct, God-given answer. The king had seen a great image whose head was of gold; arms and chest of silver; belly and thighs of brass; legs of iron, his feet part of iron and part of clay. A stone, cut out without hands, smote the image and totally destroyed it. Daniel correctly mentioned the various kingdoms to come after the Babylonian empire, namely, the Media-Persian, Grecian, and Roman, all lesser in absolute power, as the metals described, with the King being the head of gold. The stone cut out from the mountain, represents the Kingdom of God which would never end. The fourth empire, the Roman, in a revived form in the last days, is the one from which springs the last great ruler at the end of the age. As noted below, the roots of this king, his personality and purpose are found in Daniel chapter 11. Speaking of him Daniel wrote in Daniel 9:26 (KJV)

26 *"And after threescore and two weeks shall Messiah be cut off, but not for himself: and* **the people of the prince that shall come shall destroy the city and the sanctuary;** *and the end thereof shall be with a flood, and unto the end of the war desolations are determined."*

This Prince is the Antichrist who will appear on the stage after the Rapture of the saints and at the beginning of the great tribulation. Many have thought that since Rome destroyed Jerusalem in A.D 70, by Titus Vespasian, therefore antichrist comes from Rome. The people of the said Prince to come did indeed belong to the Roman army, but according to the contemporary historian Josephus, it was the Syrian and Assyrian cohorts in that army which gave the final destructive blow to Jerusalem. It is evident, therefore, that the Antichrist comes out of the north Assyrian or more exactly the Seleucid dynasty, so is properly referred to as the King of the North. Of him it is written in Daniel 8:10-11 (KJV):

10 *"And it **waxed great, even to the host of heaven**; and it cast down some of the host and of the stars to the ground, and stamped upon them.*

11 *Yea, he magnified himself even to the prince of the host, and by him the **daily sacrifice was taken away**, and the place of his sanctuary was cast down."*

As seen in the previous chapter, in the book of Daniel, chapter 11, the King of the North responds to the attack from Egypt, the King of the South; having conquered him, he goes on to establish his rule over Ethiopia and Libya, and the rest of Africa. This is doubtless what causes the Russian confederate group and the kings of the East to come up to Israel, as the Beast or Antichrist now exerts power over all the near East and so is in control of all the neighbouring oil resources, even to the Gulf of Hormuz. Evidently, the Arab world has received this conqueror and identifies him as their Mahdi, their long-expected ruler. A Prime minister of Iran, has proclaimed that they expect him to come and rule the world. It ought not to be wondered at, therefore, that Moab and Ammon are spared in his assault on Egypt. It is surely inexplicable, but shows the divine inspiration in the detail that this King of the North comes against Egypt *"with many ships."* Daniel 11:40 (KJV):

40 *" And at the time of the end shall the king of the south push at him: and the king of the north shall come against him like a **whirlwind**, with chariots, and*

*with horsemen, **and with many ships**; and he shall enter into the countries, and shall **overflow and pass over**."*

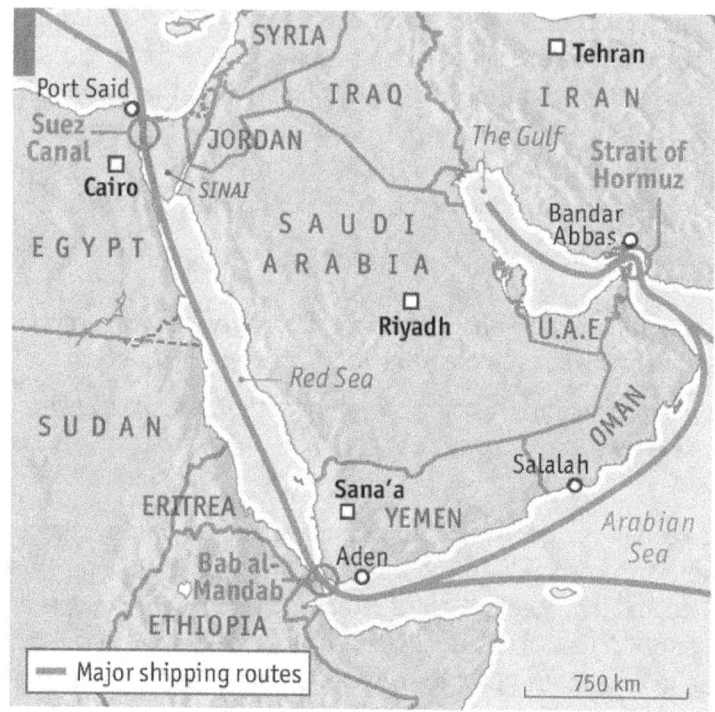

Economist.com

The Nile, due to sedimentary deposits from its source in the mountains, is not particularly known for its navigability, so there must be another reason for this fleet of ships. Obviously, Daniel himself would not have had even a clue about this, but the inspired word noted it. Today we are well aware of the Suez Canal, the gateway to the Far East, and with a ***fleet of ships***, control of the Straits of Hormuz and the entire Oil supply of the region would be in the hands of the despot known as Antichrist, the King of the North. No doubt this is good reason for the Kings of the East and the Russian confederacy from the North to come down to the battle of Armageddon, (Revelation 16: 12-14; Daniel 11:44). Earlier in this very year of 2021, the importance of the Suez Canal was seen, when for many days, ships were bottle-necked there when a oil tanker got stuck in the canal.

On line in the Internet recently, a picture of the U.S. Aircraft carrier, Dwight D. Eisenhower could be seen there in the Red Sea.

The certainty of the identification of this Assyrian is seen in Micah 5:5-6 (KJV):

*5 " And this man shall be the peace, when **the Assyrian shall come into our land**: and **when he shall tread in our palaces**, then shall we raise against him seven shepherds, and eight principal men.*

*6 And they **shall waste the land of Assyria with the sword**, and the **land of Nimrod** in the entrances thereof: **thus, shall he deliver us from the Assyrian, when he cometh into our land, and when he treadeth within our borders. "***

Again this Assyrian is referred to, whom Christ will slay with the breath of His mouth at the close of the battle of Armageddon, Isaiah 11:3-4 (KJV)

3 And shall make him of quick understanding in the fear of the LORD: and he shall not judge after the sight of his eyes, neither reprove after the hearing of his ears:

*4 " But with righteousness shall he judge the poor, and reprove with equity for the meek of the earth: and **he shall smite the earth with the rod of his mouth, and with the breath of his lips shall he slay the wicked. "***

Furthermore, this Assyrian is identified as the Antichrist in Isaiah 30:33 (KJV):

30 And the LORD shall cause his glorious voice to be heard, and shall shew the lighting down of his arm, with the indignation of his anger, and with the flame of a devouring fire, with scattering, and tempest, and hailstones.

*31 For **through the voice of the LORD shall the Assyrian be beaten down**, which smote with a rod.*

Yet again in Isaiah 30:33 (KJV)

*33 " **For Tophet is ordained of old; yea, for the king it is prepared; he hath made it deep and large: the pile thereof is fire and much wood; the breath of the LORD, like a stream of brimstone, doth kindle it. "***

The final scene of the fulfillment of these prophecies is evident today in the amalgamation of nations. The European Union forms the basis of the Old Roman empire of which Iraq, and particularly northern Iraq, the Old Assyria, formed a part and is called the King of the North, as opposed to the northern Army, from the extremities of the north, composed of Russia and her allies. It is significant that Iran, the old Persia, is currently allied with Russia; the nations of the far East are fully formed, with definite aspirations and alignment that conforms to the last days.

In the book of Zephaniah, the collusion of today's Arab and Moslem nations in claiming the land of Israel; magnifying themselves against their territory; dividing it up and hurling insults against them, are clearly seen. For this reason, the wrath and anger of the Lord is kindled against them.

Zephaniah 2:8-11 (KJV):

8 **"I have heard the reproach of Moab, and the revilings of the children of Ammon, whereby they have reproached my people,**

and magnified themselves against their border.

9 *Therefore as I live, saith the LORD of hosts, the God of Israel,* **Surely Moab shall be as Sodom, and the children of Ammon as Gomorrah,** *even the breeding of nettles, and saltpits, and a perpetual desolation: the* **residue of my people shall spoil them, and the remnant of my people shall possess them.**

10 *This shall they have for their pride,* **because they have reproached and magnified themselves against the people of the LORD of hosts.**

11 **The LORD will be terrible unto them**: *for he will famish all the gods of the earth; and men shall worship him, every one from his place, even all the isles of the heathen. "*

Gaza too will come into this judgment at the Coming of the Lord. This area next to Israel was occupied by the Philistines, from which the name Palestine, is derived. These people came as refugees from Crete after the great earthquake around 1500 B.C. In Hebrew they are called Cherethites, the word Crete being derived from the Hebrew consonants, C-r-t. Zephaniah 2:4-7 (KJV):

4 "**For Gaza shall be forsaken,** and **Ashkelon a desolation**: they shall **drive out Ashdod** at the noon day, **and Ekron shall be rooted up.**

5 **Woe unto the inhabitants of the sea coast, the nation of the Cherethites**! the word of the LORD is against you; O Canaan, the land of the Philistines, I will even destroy thee, that there shall be no inhabitant.

6 And the sea coast shall be dwellings and cottages for shepherds, and folds for flocks.

7 And **the coast shall be for the remnant of the house of Judah**; they shall feed thereupon: in the houses of Ashkelon shall they lie down in the evening: for the LORD their God shall visit them, and turn away their captivity."

Events, therefore, of the past few years are all indications that this is the end time, and all the nations are lining up, exactly in the way the prophets predicted in the Scriptures.

It is not without significance, therefore, that in identifying the cities and nations, in Isaiah chapter 34, the names of Bozra, the chief city of the Edomites, is named. Moab, Idumea, and Tophet are also mentioned among the places of destruction at the time of the day of vengeance of the Lord, when the heavens are rolled back and the land is in flames. These peoples and lands are identified today as Moslem and Arabs. Linking Daniel's prophecy in chapter 11, with these prophecies of Isaiah, it can readily be seen that Antichrist, having conquered Egypt, and hearing of the movement of the Kings of the East and of Russia from the north, hurries back to Israel, having great wrath and destruction in mind. He is met in Tophet, on the Lord's return, and there he meets his end. It can be seen that at the return of Christ this army of Antichrist, returning from Africa, meet their end. Habakkuk 3:3-9 (KJV):

3 *"God came from Teman, and the Holy One from mount Paran. Selah. His glory covered the heavens, and the earth was full of his praise.*

4 *And his brightness was as the light; he had horns coming out of his hand: and there was the hiding of his power.*

5 **Before him went the pestilence, and burning coals went forth at his feet.**

6 *He stood, and measured the earth: he beheld, and **drove asunder the nations**; and the everlasting mountains were scattered, the perpetual hills did bow: his ways are everlasting.*

7 *I saw the **tents of Cushan in affliction**: and the curtains of **the land of Midian did tremble**.*

8 *Was the LORD displeased against the rivers? was thine anger against the rivers? was thy wrath against the sea, that thou didst ride upon thine horses and thy chariots of salvation?*

9 *Thy bow was made quite naked, according to the oaths of the tribes, even thy word. Selah."*

All these denominations of southern nations explain why the coming of the Lord centers on this area, where the armies of Antichrist are located in their return to Israel, and culminates on the Mount of Olives, which is before Jerusalem. It is significant too, that antichrist is destroyed by the breath of the Lord in Tophet, the valley south of Jerusalem.

Israel will have taken refuge at Petra, so the Lord, like the lightening, coming from the East to the West, will come to this area in the deliverance and protection of His people.

CHAPTER 7

HEAVEN & EARTH IN JUDGMENT

In all the Scriptures there is a symbiotic (from Greek, συμ-, *together, with; βιος, life,* = *living together*) relationship between the earth and the heavens. There is no earth without its heavens and vice versa. The word *heaven,* in Hebrew signifies, *waters above.* It is not at all surprising that the Scriptures commence with the words, *In the beginning God created the heavens and the earth.* The relationship between the two entities, between God in Heaven and man on earth, made in His own image, is what life and the Bible is all about. Continually, throughout this wonderful book, one's attention is drawn to this relationship, as seen in Isaiah 51:6-8 (KJV):

6 "*Lift up your **eyes to the heavens,** and **look upon the earth** beneath: **for the heavens shall vanish away like smoke, and the earth shall wax old like a garment,** and they that dwell therein shall die in like manner: **but my salvation shall be for ever, and my righteousness shall not be abolished.***

7 *Hearken **unto me,** ye that know righteousness, the people in whose heart is my law; fear ye not the reproach of men, neither be ye afraid of their revilings.* 8 *For the moth shall eat them up like a garment, and the worm shall eat them like wool: but **my righteousness shall be for ever, and my salvation from generation to generation.***"In this passage the focus is on the Coming of the Lord, exactly as noted in 2 Peter 3:1-2 (KJV):

1 "*This second epistle, beloved, I now write unto you; in both which **I stir up your pure minds by way of remembrance:***

2 *That ye may be **mindful of the words** which were **spoken before by the holy prophets,** and of the commandment of us the apostles of the Lord and Saviour:* "

The central theme of this chapter of Peter clearly sets forth the coming judgments on the ungodly at the time of Christ's coming, not at the end of the Millennium period as discussed above. The human frailty of forgetfulness and disobedience to the word of the Almighty above is recorded in Isaiah 55:6-11 (KJV):

6 " *Seek* ye the LORD while he may be found, **call ye upon him** while he is near:

7 Let the wicked forsake his way, and the **unrighteous man his thoughts**: and let him return unto the LORD, and he will have mercy upon him; and to our God, for he will abundantly pardon.

8 **For my thoughts are not your thoughts, neither are your ways my ways, saith the LORD.**

9 **For as the heavens are higher than the earth, so are my ways higher than your ways, and my thoughts than your thoughts.**

10 For as the rain cometh down, and the snow from heaven, and returneth not thither, but watereth the earth, and maketh it bring forth and bud, that it may give seed to the sower, and bread to the eater:

11 **So shall my word be that goeth forth out of my mouth: it shall not return unto me void,** but it shall **accomplish that which I please, and it shall prosper** in the thing where to I sent it."

Because of these weaknesses of man, and in contrast to God's goodness and longsuffering patience, man is not destroyed but is clearly warned in His eternal Word of the judgments and consequences which will **befall mankind and earth and heaven** through ungodly, wicked behaviour. Just as such physical consequences as Aids and venereal disease come through man's immorality; so too plagues, earthquakes in diverse places; the sea and the waves roaring in such acts as the multiplicity of hurricanes with their disastrous results, in like manner, great tribulation and unthinkable destruction shall precede the coming of Christ to destroy the ungodly, as seen in the Book of the Revelation. This book is replete with such descriptions. Christ himself warned that the days before his coming would be comparable to those of Noah's Flood and the destruction of Sodom and Gomorrah. It would seem evident today, in the light of the fulfillment of such prophecies as Israel returning to her land; the upheavals of nature and man's wicked excesses; that Covid-19, may very well be a warning shot fired across the bow of all nations!

Throughout the Bible, over and over again, attention is called to the heavens and to all things in the earth. Without doubt the most alarming call, greater even than the warnings of the Flood and its destruction, is the call announcing the return of Christ at the close of the Great Tribulation. This coming destruction is greater far than at Noah's Flood; more severe as fire is from water; a complete annihilation of the ungodly in the earth with the passing of the heavens; and in the creation of a New Heaven and a New Earth, wherein dwelleth righteousness. Many of the prophets, especially Isaiah and Joel, give unearthly descriptions of the momentous events which are coming on the earth and in the heavens at the Appearing and Revelation of Christ in flaming fire taking vindication on all the ungodly and rebellious. It is not, therefore, surprising that Peter (2 Peter 3:17) would warn of the necessity of keeping one's guard up against any ideas or teaching that would make one let down their watch, stumble, or be deceived as to the urgency of this coming judgment. This today, is the most important subject as crises multiply and iniquity abounds on all hands.

Perhaps the most descriptive passage in this connection is that from which Peter quotes in chapter three of his second epistle; it is found in Isaiah 34:1-6 (KJV):

*1 **Come near, ye nations, to hear;** and **hearken, ye people: let the earth hear, and all that is therein; the world, and all things that come forth of it.***

*2 For the **indignation of the LORD is upon all nations,** and his fury upon all their armies: **he hath utterly destroyed them,** he hath delivered them to the slaughter.*

3 Their slain also shall be cast out, and their stink shall come up out of their carcases, and the mountains shall be melted with their blood.

*4 And **all the host of heaven shall be dissolved, and the heavens shall be rolled together as a scroll: and all their host shall fall down**, as the leaf falleth off from the vine, and as a falling fig from the fig tree.*

*5 For **my sword shall be bathed in heaven**: behold, it shall come down upon **Idumea,** and upon the people of my curse, **to judgment.***

*6 The sword of the LORD is filled with blood, it is made fat with fatness, and with the blood of lambs and goats, with the fat of the kidneys of rams: for the LORD hath a **sacrifice in Bozrah**, and a great slaughter in the land of **Idumea**.*

In comparison to 2 Peter 3, it is clear that this dissolving of the heavens and destruction on the earth happen at the identical time, that is, at the coming of the Lord at the commencement of the Great and terrible day of the Lord mentioned in Joel. These are not two different judgments with 1,000 years between, as some affirm. As previously noted only **the dead** stand before Christ at the great white throne judgment; the living then at the end of the millennium period, are all righteous for the earth had already been judged at Christ's coming. A new heaven and a new earth had been recreated then, " wherein dwelleth righteousness."

A graphic account of the judgment of the living ungodly at Christ's return is found in Revelation 14:14-20 (KJV):

*14 " And I looked, and behold a white cloud, and upon the cloud **one sat like unto the Son of man**, having on his head a golden crown, and in **his hand a sharp sickle**.*

*15 And another angel came out of the temple, crying with a loud voice to him that sat on the cloud, **thrust in thy sickle, and reap**: for the time is come for thee to reap; for the **harvest of the earth is ripe**.*

16 And he that sat on the cloud thrust in his sickle on the earth; and the earth was reaped.

17 And another angel came out of the temple which is in heaven, he also having a sharp sickle.

*18 And another angel came out from the altar, which had power over fire; and cried with a loud cry to him that had the sharp sickle, saying, **thrust in thy sharp sickle, and gather the clusters of the vine of the earth; for her grapes are fully ripe.***

*19 And the angel thrust in his sickle into the earth, and gathered the vine of the earth, and **cast it into the great winepress of the***

wrath of God.

*20 And the winepress was trodden without the city, and **blood came out of the winepress, even unto the horse bridles, by the space of a thousand and six hundred furlongs.** "*

This is a description of the judgments during the great tribulation which ends in the coming of the Lord in glory with myriads of his holy angels and all his saints from the beginning with Adam to the rapture of the saints who are alive at his coming. This description is found in Zechariah 14:2-4 (KJV):

*2 "For I will **gather all nations against Jerusalem to battle**; and the city shall be taken, and the houses rifled, and the women ravished; and half of the city shall go forth into captivity, and the residue of the people shall not be cut off from the city.*

*3 Then shall the **LORD go forth, and fight against those nations,** as when he fought in the day of battle.*

*4 And **his feet shall stand in that day** upon the mount of Olives, which is before Jerusalem on the east, and the mount of Olives shall cleave in the midst thereof toward the east and toward the west, and there shall be a very great valley; and half of the mountain shall remove toward the north, and half of it toward the south. "* The result of this battle is the total destruction of the oppressors as noted further in Zechariah 14:12-13 (KJV):

*12 "And this shall be the **plague wherewith the LORD will smite all the people** that have fought against Jerusalem; **Their flesh shall consume away while they stand upon their feet, and their eyes shall consume away in their holes, and their tongue shall consume away in their mouth.***

13 And it shall come to pass in that day, that a great tumult from the LORD shall be among them; and they shall lay hold every one on the hand of his neighbour, and his hand shall rise up against the hand of his neighbour."

This will bring an end to the great tribulation; the remaining nations will come before the Lord for judgment and allocation to the Kingdom on earth called the millennium or to destruction, as noted previously.

CHAPTER 8

THE KINGDOM OF GOD--NEW HEAVEN & NEW EARTH

Christ said to the Jews: John 3:12 (KJV):

*12 "If I have told you **earthly things**, and **ye believe not**, how shall ye believe, if I tell you of **heavenly** things? "*

This is the conundrum today. Most of the world does not know the God who created the heavens and the earth; many deny his very existence and are not interested in knowing about heavenly things, but are only living for what they can see and touch. To such the veil of darkness covers all the future. This present world is under the influence of the rulers of this darkness, as the works of the flesh are clearly manifest in their lives. The coming Kingdom of God, for which all the Apostles preached and looked, as well as the Jews, is beyond the comprehension of most people and if told they would not believe it either.

It stretches mortal imagination to comprehend earthly things, how much more the heavenly? Nevertheless, for the spiritual man, the veil has been partially removed and from the scriptures, the future can be gloriously embraced. This coming Kingdom of God has ever been the focus of God, even before the Fall of man, and the creation of the world.

Christ Jesus will say to the nations on his right hand at the judgment of the nations at his coming: Matthew 25:34 (KJV):

*34 " Then shall the King say unto them on his right hand, Come, **ye blessed** of my Father, **inherit** the **kingdom prepared** for you **from the foundation of the world:** "*

It is certain that this kingdom is not this present one, encountered at his Coming, so any talk of a dissolution and burning up at the end of the Millennial reign of Christ is not feasible as the Kingdom, prepared from the foundation of the world *"cannot be moved"*, and is not dissolvable! The Kingdom to which Christ refers is the one that is created at his coming, when as noted in 2 Peter 3:10-13, the heavens pass away; the works of men are burnt up; unto which fire the earth was kept and treasured up; the elements burn with fervent heat; and a new heaven and a new earth, wherein dwelleth righteousness, such as the Apostles intimated, are then created, as noted in Isaiah chapters 65:17-20 and 66. Here are some of the characteristics of this new heaven and new earth at the start of the millennial reign of Christ. In chapter 65:16, 17, the troubles, anguish, anxieties from the Fall, (the Hebrew original uses the same word for "In the beginning," that is, at the head of things), all that has been afflicted on mankind, will be lifted to a great degree; man's past sins will be forgotten by God; will not even come up in the heart of man, but will be replaced by joy and rejoicing in the soul and heart, as stated in Isaiah 65:16-18 (KJV):

*16 "That he who blesseth himself in the earth **shall bless himself in the God of truth**; and he that sweareth in the earth shall swear by the God of truth; **because the former troubles are forgotten**, and because **they are hid from mine eyes.***

*17 For, **behold, I create new heavens and a new earth**: and the former **shall not be remembered, nor come into mind.***

*18 But be ye glad and rejoice for ever in that which I create: for, **behold, I create Jerusalem a rejoicing**, and **her people a joy."***

This is the first great blessing: forgiveness and forgetting of the past. The next is that the soul, spirit, and body are fully filled with unutterable joy, continually. Not only man but God the Creator, shall joy in Jerusalem and his people Israel. This kingdom was promised to the friend of God, Abraham; to his seed Isaac; to Jacob, renamed Israel; and through Judah to the house of David, whose descendant, Christ, would reign forever over this Kingdom. This was the focal hope of Jewry, whose name and exaltation among the gentile nations, will abide forever. As stated in Isaiah 66:22, proves the eternity of the new heaven and new earth:

*22 "For **as the new heavens and the new earth,** which I will make, **shall remain before me,** saith the LORD, so shall **your seed and your name remain. "***

This Kingdom is not a mere earthly kingdom, but an eternal one. As Christ said to the Jews in Luke 17:21 (KJV):

*21 "Neither shall they say, Lo here! or, lo there! for, behold, **the kingdom of God is within you.** "*

Again, it is evident that this kingdom which begins at the reign of Christ at the beginning of the millennium, with the transformation of the present age and its heaven and earth, into a new one, will never pass away or come into dissolution. In Revelation 21:1, therefore, the Apostle John, writing and experiencing the vision on the isle of Patmos, near the end of the first Century, was looking back from the point in his revelation to this new heaven and earth as he explained that the first heaven and earth (in which both he and we now live), had passed away and there was no more sea. He was looking at the same kingdom that came into being at the Coming of Christ when the living ungodly were judged and destroyed as noted previously. Any supposition that yet another new heaven and new earth would be suddenly formed and the then existing kingdom pass away is clearly ill-conceived and erroneous, though it is understandable from a superficial reading of the text.

The description of the New Heaven and New Earth of Isaiah 65 and 66, describes the changes that come into this new age as it affects animals, the life expectancy of man, indeed the drastic changes in life itself. Isaiah well expresses this in Isaiah 2:2-4 (KJV):

*2 "And it shall come to pass **in the last days,** that the mountain of the LORD'S house shall be established in the top of the mountains, and shall be exalted above the hills; and all nations shall flow unto it.*

*3 And many people shall go and say, Come ye, and let us go up to the mountain of the LORD, to the house of the God of Jacob; and **he will teach us of his ways, and we will walk in his paths: for out of Zion shall go forth the law, and the word of the LORD from Jerusalem.***

⁴ And he shall judge among the nations, and shall rebuke many people: and they shall beat their swords into plowshares, and their spears into pruninghooks: nation shall not lift up sword against nation, neither shall they learn war any more."

Also, as to the creation, as seen in Isaiah 11:4-10 (KJV):

*⁴ But with **righteousness** shall he judge the poor, and reprove with equity for the meek of the earth: and he shall smite the earth with the rod of his mouth, and with the **breath of his lips shall he slay the wicked.***

⁵ And righteousness shall be the girdle of his loins, and faithfulness the girdle of his reins.

*⁶ **The wolf also shall dwell with the lamb,** and the **leopard shall lie down with the kid;** and the **calf and the young lion** and the fatling together; and **a little child shall lead them.***

*⁷ And the **cow and the bear shall feed; their young ones shall lie down together**: and the **lion shall eat straw like the ox.***

*⁸ And the **sucking child shall play on the hole of the asp,** and the **weaned child shall put his hand on the cockatrice' den.***

*⁹ **They shall not hurt nor destroy in all my holy mountain**: for the **earth shall be full of the knowledge of the LORD**, as the waters cover the sea.*

¹⁰ And in that day, there shall be a root of Jesse, which shall stand for an ensign of the people; to it shall the Gentiles seek: and his rest shall be glorious.

This Kingdom of God in the millennial age, the Palingenesis mentioned by Christ in Matthew 19:28, will then be composed of the nations, found on the right hand of Christ in Matthew 25; the transformed saints raptured before the tribulation; the Old Testament saints, as noted in Daniel 12, who himself shall stand in his lot in those days; and indeed all the saints from Adam, including Noah, Abraham, Isaac, Jacob, Moses and others; all the prophets of old, including of course Isaiah, and all who came after. What a congregation of saints, what a reunion of the blessed!

In the words of the prophet Isaiah 4:2-5 (KJV):

2 "*In that day shall the **branch of the LORD be beautiful and glorious,** and the **fruit of the earth shall be excellent and comely** for them that are escaped of Israel.*

3 *And it shall come to pass, that he that is left in Zion, and he that remaineth in Jerusalem, **shall be called holy,** even every one that is written among the living in Jerusalem:*

4 *When the Lord shall have washed away the filth of the daughters of Zion, and shall have **purged the blood** of Jerusalem from the midst thereof by the **spirit of judgment,** and by the **spirit of burning.***

5 *And **the LORD will create upon every dwelling place of mount Zion,** and upon her assemblies, **a cloud and smoke by day**, and the **shining of a flaming fire by night**: for upon all the glory shall be a defence.*

6 *And there **shall be a tabernacle for a shadow in the daytime from the heat,** and for a **place of refuge,** and for a **covert from storm and from rain."***

These latter verses are a fitting recapitulation of Exodus 13:21-22 (KJV):

21 " *And the LORD went before them by day in a **pillar of a cloud, to lead them the way;** and **by night in a pillar of fire, to give them light;** to go by day and night:*

22 *He took not away the pillar of the cloud by day, nor the pillar of fire by night, from before the people."*

In the wilderness journey there were no electric lights, no street lights and not an abundance of oil. It was a new way, untrodden by all but Moses. There would doubtless be danger from wild beasts, hostile people and tribes, and the pillar of cloud by day would guide them in the way, the pillar of fire by night would light up the surrounding darkness, but above all give the assurance of the Presence and power of the Lord who had delivered them from Egypt and safely crossed the Red Sea. This is the joyful assurance that the people in the new kingdom will experience. Moreover, the exalted Lord, being their God and Saviour would complete their joy and glory as expressed in Isaiah 28:5-6 (KJV):

5 "In that day shall the **LORD of hosts** be for a **crown of glory,** and for a **diadem of beauty**, unto the residue of his people,

6 And for a **spirit of judgment** to him that sitteth in judgment, and for strength to them that turn the battle to the gate."

All will be renewed and filled with joyfulness, as seen in Isaiah 29:18-19 (KJV):

18 "And in that day shall the **deaf hear the words of the book**, and the **eyes of the blind shall see** out of obscurity, and out of darkness.

19 The **meek also shall increase their joy in the LORD**, and the poor among men **shall rejoice in the Holy One of Israel."**

The whole purpose of the creation of heaven and earth and all in them, is to reveal in a physical, living, and eternal way the innate glory, love, righteousness, holiness, and omnipotence of the unseen God who dwells in light unapproachable. This is partially expressed thus in Isaiah 5:16 (KJV):

16 "But the LORD of hosts shall be **exalted in judgment**, and **God that is holy shall be sanctified in righteousness**."

The physical results are noted in Isaiah 35:5-10 (KJV):

5 "Then the eyes of the blind shall be opened, and the ears of the deaf shall be unstopped.

*⁶ Then shall the **lame man leap as an hart**, and the tongue of **the dumb sing:** for in the **wilderness shall waters break out,** and **streams in the desert.***

*⁷ And the **parched ground shall become a pool,** and the **thirsty land springs of water:** in the habitation of dragons, where each lay, shall **be grass with reeds** and rushes.*

*⁸ And a **highway shall be there, and a way,** and it shall be called **the way of holiness;** the unclean shall not pass over it; but it shall be for those: the wayfaring men, though fools, shall not err therein.*

⁹ No lion shall be there, nor any ravenous beast shall go up thereon, it shall not be found there; but the redeemed shall walk there:

*¹⁰ And the **ransomed of the LORD** shall return, and **come to Zion with songs and everlasting joy** upon their heads: **they shall obtain joy and gladness, and sorrow and sighing shall flee away. "***

Then our earthly song will echo as in the song of A.H. Ashley and music of B.D. Ashley:

Days are filled with gladness, nights are filled with song, Walking in the King's highway;

And the world goes brighter, as we pass along, Walking in the King's highway.

Chorus:

Walking, walking in the King's highway, To the place of many

mansions, I shall meet at last, Walking in the King's highway.

Music from the homeland fills me with delight, Walking in the King's highway:

Visions of the glory break upon my sight, Walking in the King's highway.

Crown'd with tender mercies, guarded by his love, Walking in the King's highway,

Jesus gives a foretaste of the joys above, Walking in the King's highway.

CHAPTER 9

THE ALPHA & OMEGA ON THE THRONE

The visible creation calls for a visible Crown and Head. Perhaps this is the reason for the creation of man in the image and likeness of God. He who sits on the throne above all, declares in Psalm 89:13-14 (KJV):

13"Thou hast a mighty arm: strong is thy hand, and high is thy right hand.
*14 Justice **and judgment** are the **habitation of thy throne**: mercy and truth shall go before thy face."*

And again, in Isaiah 9:19:

*19 Through the wrath of the LORD of hosts is the land darkened, and the **people** shall be as the **fuel of the fire**: no man shall spare his brother.*

Regardless of where it is found, all iniquity must be judged. This concept seems foreign to many who wonder why eternal punishment is dispensed for ever on the lost soul. It is simply that the soul is eternal and the choice is theirs. Anyone, therefore, that rejects the pro-offered Saviour will bear their own judgment. The horrors and calamities that come on the ungodly are the just anger of *our God* who *is a consuming fire* and *is of purer eyes than to behold iniquity and canst not look upon sin.*

For this reason, the prophet Isaiah relates to Israel and Jerusalem the judgments of God and the tribulation that comes upon them, even by the nations that surround them. Be assured though that their God will judge those nations with the fire of his wrath. The joyous end will be the restoration of Jerusalem, but only a remnant, one-third, will come through the fire of judgment.

Alpha and Omega are the first and last letters of the Greek Alphabet, in other words, all their language is contained within them. Christ, in similitude, is the Beginning and End of all, in the words of the Apostle Paul in Colossians 2:8-10:

8 "Beware lest any man spoil you through philosophy and vain deceit, after the tradition of men, after the rudiments of the world, and not after Christ.

9 For in him dwelleth all the fulness of the Godhead bodily.

10 And ye are complete in him, which is the head of all principality and power: "

And again, in Revelation 1:8 (KJV):

8 "I am Alpha and Omega, the beginning and the ending, saith the Lord, which is, and which was, and which is to come, the Almighty."

It is to Him, therefore, that all might, majesty dominion and power, in heaven and earth, are committed as noted in Hebrews 1:1-3:

1 "God, who at sundry times and in divers manners spake in time past unto the fathers by the prophets,

*2 Hath in these last days spoken unto us by his Son, whom **he hath appointed heir of all things**, by **whom also he made the worlds;***

*3 Who being the brightness of his glory, and the express image of his person, and upholding all things by the word of his power, when he had by **himself purged our sins, sat down on the right hand of the Majesty on high; "***

The throne of the Kingdom of God is referred to by Christ as "*the throne of glory*" *(Matthew 19:28; 25:31),* and this will take place at his Coming and will endure for a thousand years on earth. Then the New Jerusalem will come down to earth and God will dwell with man forever.

This is well expressed by Isaac Watts' Hymn (Hursley 273):

Jesus shall reign where'er the sun, Doth his successive journey's run;

His kingdom stretch from shore to shore, Till suns shall rise and set no more.

Peoples and realms of every tongue, Dwell on his love with sweetest song;

And infant voices shall proclaim, their young hosannas to his name.

Blessings abound where'er he reigns; The prisoner leaps to lose his

chains; The weary find eternal rest, And all the sons of want are blest.

Where he displays his healing power, Death and the curse are known no more;

In him the tribes of Adam boast, more blessings than their

father lost. Let every creature rise and bring, Its grateful honors

to our king; Angels descend with songs again, and earth prolong

the joyful strain.

What Christ Jesus has accomplished is to put a man at the very right hand of God, by himself taking on the seed of Adam and Abraham, and becoming the propitiation for our sins, restore man to a place of honor where God can again delight in him. This is a feat that could only originate and be accomplished in the loving, forgiving heart of God. By such actions the universe of powers, angels and men get a glimpse of the very heart and nature of the Almighty.

CHAPTER 10

SUMMARY OF VISIONS AND END TIME

A most astounding promise and characteristic of the Scriptures is that God, the Creator and upholder of Heaven and earth, does nothing without first intimating to His servants, the prophets, what He will do. Amos 3:7 (KJV)

7 Surely the Lord GOD will do nothing, but he revealeth his secret unto his servants the prophets.

This principle flows throughout Scripture and the more amazing and wondrous the deed, the more frequently is it reiterated throughout the Word. The method of communication may vary, but the Word is clear, whether in a vision, by the spoken word, or in the Spirit, in diverse ways and places (Hebrews 1:1). The coming of Christ into the world to destroy the devil and redeem mankind, begins in Genesis 3:16, at the expulsion of the primal pair from Eden. Innumerable scriptures and details are given throughout by the prophets and messengers of God, so that the divine message could not be clearer. The miraculous birth, place, manner, time, are all given centuries before. Details like the crucifixion, unknown in David's time, some 1,000 years before; the parting of His garments and casting lots for His outer garment (the seamless robe of John 19:24); the very words that the people uttered at the cross, are all given in Psalm 22. Isaiah 53 describes the scene and explains the purpose, the substitutionary nature of Christ's death and resurrection, on man's behalf. The coming Return of Christ in glory, as Lord of all; judge of all in the fire of God's wrath; the destruction of billions of people, animals, cities of earth, will surely be the greatest manifestation of God's glory, power, majesty that has ever been displayed.

In the book of Habakkuk, as seen earlier, this vision is given and foretold. As could be expected, this wondrous event is repeated in the prophecies and in Habakkuk, in which it is clearly described as a vision, which, though it tarries will surely come to pass. The background of this vision is based on the prophet's own experience and times which fittingly reflect the terrible future and wrath as God returns to vindicate His word.

In chapter 3:1,2, and the first word of Psalm 7, Shigionoth signifies a loud, vigorous, impassioned, aboundingly triumphant hymn of praise extolling God. Both in this title and in the verses of Psalm 7:6, 9, & 11, and in the body of this poem, are expressed the great **judgment of God** in wiping out sin and **establishing righteousness,** embracing His people, cleansing and purifying the world. Psalm 7:6 (KJV)

6 "*Arise, O LORD, in thine anger,* lift up thyself because of the rage of mine enemies: and *awake for me to the judgment that thou hast commanded. "Psalm 7:8-9 (KJV)*

8 The **LORD shall judge the people: judge me, O LORD, according to my righteousness,** and according to mine integrity that is in me.

9 Oh let the **wickedness of the wicked come to an end; but establish the just: for the righteous God** trieth the hearts and reins.

Habakkuk 1:12-13 (KJV)

12 Art thou not from everlasting, O LORD my God, mine Holy One? we shall not die. **O LORD, thou hast ordained them for judgment;** and, O mighty God, **thou hast established them for correction.**

13 Thou art of purer eyes than to behold evil, and **canst not look on iniquity:**

Habakkuk 3:12-13 (KJV)

12 Thou **didst march through the land in indignation, thou didst thresh the heathen in anger.**

13 Thou **wentest forth for the salvation of thy people, even for salvation with thine anointed; thou woundedst the head out of the house of the wicked, by discovering the foundation unto the neck. Selah.**

The Hebrew name Habakkuk means *embrace.* The title to this vision in chapter 3:1, is:

1 "*A **prayer of Habakkuk** the prophet **upon Shigionoth.**"*The most glorious, earth shaking, upheaval of heaven and earth is about to be announced and described by the prophet. The Apostle John, writing about 750 years later, expressed in Revelation 19:1-6, the reason for the shouts of praise and acclamation given at this time of Christ's return in this portion:

1 "*And after these things I heard a great voice of much people in heaven, saying, Alleluia; Salvation, and glory, and honour, and power, unto the Lord our God:*

2 *For true and righteous are his judgments: for he hath judged the great whore, which did corrupt the earth with her fornication, and hath avenged the blood of his servants at her hand.*
3 *And again they said, Alleluia. And her smoke rose up for ever and ever.*"

In verse 2 of chapter 3, Habakkuk looks forward to this coming of the Lord, the most glorious, stupendous, and amazing event since man was on the earth; he reflects on the whole Word of God; the prophecies and the promises, writing: "*O LORD, I have heard thy speech, and was afraid:*"In the translation of this phrase from Hebrew much is lost.

The word *speech, and heard,* are the same root word, and would be clearer had it been translated: "O Lord, *I **heard** thy **report** (renown, fame) and **was afraid.**" The words of Isaiah would then come to mind, Isaiah 53:1-9 (KJV):

1 *Who hath believed **our report**? and to whom is the **arm of the LORD revealed?***
2 *For he shall grow up before him as a tender plant, and as a root out of a dry ground: he hath no form nor comeliness; and when we shall see him, there is no beauty that we should desire him.*

3 He is despised and rejected of men; a man of sorrows, and acquainted with grief: and we hid as it were our faces from him; **he was despised, and we esteemed him not.**

4 Surely, he hath borne our griefs, and carried our sorrows: yet we did esteem him stricken, smitten of God, and afflicted.

5 But he was wounded for our transgressions, he was bruised for our iniquities: the chastisement of our peace was upon him; and with his stripes we are healed.

6 All we like sheep have gone astray; we have turned everyone to his own way; and the LORD hath laid on him the iniquity of us all.

7 He was oppressed, and he was afflicted, yet he opened not his mouth: he is brought as a lamb to the slaughter, and as a sheep before her shearers is dumb, so he openeth not his mouth.

8 He was taken from prison and from judgment: and who shall declare his generation? for he was cut off out of the land of the living: for the transgression of my people was he stricken.

9 And he made his grave with the wicked, and with the rich in his death; because he had done no violence, neither was any deceit in his mouth.

The proof of this lies in comparing the Hebrew in which most words use 3 or 4 consonants to give the basic meaning of a word. Prefixes, infixes, and suffixes enlarge or lessen the meaning etc. Compare the two passages first in Isaiah 53:1, and then in Habakkuk 3:2 *in Hebrew,* the 3 letters representing ***hear, report*** are in bold.

מי האמין ל**שמע**תנו וזרוע יהוה על־מי נגלתה: ב

יהוה **שמע**תי **שמע**ך יראתי

The ***report*** then is clearly the evangelical gospel of Christ coming to suffer and die and rise again to give life and salvation to mankind. This is the theme throughout all Scripture. Those rejecting it will suffer great loss and judgment. This then is what causes the prophet to be afraid of what is coming on the earth. The message of Christ's coming in judgment, avenging his words and warnings, contrast with the great humiliation, shame, suffering and indignities heaped upon Him, for whom, by whom, and through whom all exist and subsist. He whom the world despised and rejected is now glorified, exalted above all. Christ's position then will be the very antithesis of what it was on earth in the days of His flesh. In the words of the hymn writer, "The head that once was crowned with thorns is crowned with glory now, a royal diadem adorns the mighty victor's brow."

He is the Divine Lord of all, resplendent in the glory of heaven; the appointed judge and executor of the will of God in wiping out wickedness and establishing righteousness in all the earth and universe.

This contrast and wonder of Divine love reaching down to the lowest depth to save rebellious man, exalting him to heavenly heights, certainly evokes the highest wonder, glory and praise that man can feel or express. The prophet expresses such emotions speaking of rottenness in his bones and inner being in the presence of so great a Lord and Saviour.

Habakkuk, in this chapter, more so than all the prophets before or after him, describes the results of what John saw in Revelation 19, namely, the return of Christ from heaven to earth, in the day of vengeance, destruction of ungodly men, and the formation of a new heaven and new earth where Christ reigns supreme. John wrote: Revelation 19:5-6 (KJV)

5"And a voice came out of the throne, saying, Praise our God, all ye his servants, and ye that fear him, both small and great.

*6And I heard as it were the **voice of a great multitude,** and a**s the voice of many waters, and as the voice of mighty thunderings, saying, Alleluia: for the Lord God omnipotent reigneth."***

Revelation 19:11-18 (KJV)

*11"And I saw heaven opened, and behold a white horse; and he that sat upon him was called Faithful and True, and **in righteousness he doth judge and make war.***

*12**His eyes were as a flame of fire, and on his head were many crowns;** and he had a name written, that no man knew, but he himself.*

*13And he was c**lothed with a vesture dipped in blood: and his name is called The Word of God.***

14And the armies which were in heaven followed him upon white horses, clothed in fine linen, white and clean.

15And out of his mouth goeth a sharp sword, that with it he should smite the nations: and he shall rule them with a rod of iron: and he treadeth the winepress of the fierceness and wrath of Almighty God.

[16]And he hath on his vesture and on his thigh a name written, KING OF KINGS, AND LORD OF LORDS.

[17]And I saw an angel standing in the sun; and he cried with a loud voice, saying to all the fowls that fly in the midst of heaven, Come and gather yourselves together unto the supper of the great God;

[18]That ye may eat the flesh of kings, and the flesh of captains, and the flesh of mighty men, and the flesh of horses, and of them that sit on them, and the flesh of all men, both free and bond, both small and great."

Habakkuk reveals what happens on earth in this portion of chapter 3:3-7 (previously quoted in chapter 7):

Habakkuk 3:3-19 (KJV)

[3] God came from Teman, and the Holy One from mount Paran. Selah. His glory covered the heavens, and the earth was full of his praise.

[4] And his brightness was as the light; he had horns coming out of his hand: and there was the hiding of his power.

[5] Before him went the pestilence, and burning coals went forth at his feet.

[6] He stood, and measured the earth: he beheld, and drove asunder the nations; and the everlasting mountains were scattered, the perpetual hills did bow: his ways are everlasting.

[7] I saw the tents of Cushan in affliction: and the curtains of the land of Midian did tremble.

To understand this passage, and indeed this the greatest intervention of God in history, save only by that of Christ's sufferings, crucifixion and resurrection, it is expedient to compare it with Isaiah's prophecy of this same event. **Isaiah 34:3-10 (KJV)**

*[3]Their slain also shall be cast out, and their stink shall come up out of their carcases, and **the mountains shall be melted with their blood.***

*[4]**And all the host of heaven shall be dissolved, and the heavens shall be rolled together as a scroll: and all their host shall fall down,** as the leaf falleth off from the vine, and as a falling fig from the fig tree.*

*[5]**For my sword shall be bathed in heaven: behold, it shall come down upon Idumea, and upon the people of my curse, to judgment.***

*6The sword of the LORD is filled with blood, it is made fat with fatness, and with the blood of lambs and goats, with the fat of the kidneys of rams: for the **LORD hath a sacrifice in Bozrah, and a great slaughter in the land of Idumea.***

7And the unicorns shall come down with them, and the bullocks with the bulls; and their land shall be soaked with blood, and their dust made fat with fatness.

*8**For it is the day of the LORD'S vengeance, and the year of recompences for the controversy of Zion.***

*9And the streams thereof shall be turned into pitch, and the dust thereof into brimstone, and the **land thereof shall become burning pitch.***

*10It shall not be quenched night nor day; **the smoke thereof shall go up for ever**: from generation to generation, it shall lie waste; none shall pass through it for ever and ever.*

Bosra the capital of Idumea, lies south and east of the land of Israel, as does Teman, the land of the Cushites, Ethiopia, and Midia, and Petra. From Daniel 11:40 to 44, the King of the North (Seleucid dynasty), Antichrist no doubt, is attacking Egypt and conquers all the area and hears news of the Kings of the east and north coming to Meggido in Israel. The remnant third of Israel had taken refuge in Petra and Christ returns to this area to rescue His people and destroy His enemies. He comes with all his saints and angelic armies of heaven, from this south eastern area and as the lightning goes from east to west, so His brightness, glory, and power, overwhelm all. Lightning is but a momentary flash in contrast to the sustained brilliance of Christ's appearance at His coming. It is at this time that the **day of vengeance begins** with the rolling back of the heavens; the epochal changes of the heavens; the earth and the seas churn in motion, as Christ returns in flames of fire. The prophet Habakkuk describes and names Teman meaning *right,* as in Hebrew, *the right hand,* being south and east of the land of Israel. This is the area conquered by Antichrist as seen above. Christ is described in Isaiah 34, as having garments dipped in the blood of His enemies. The magnitude of His coming is world-wide, not only are the heavens rolled away with a great hissing noise, as expressed in above passage of Isaiah and in 2 Peter 3:10, but the deep sea, the abyss, in Hebrew called *tohum,* is lifted up on high, thus forming a new heaven. This lifting up of the deep would cause catastrophic reverberations on earth as the seas, rising upward, would take pressure off from the tectonic plates causing them to return to their former positions. The high mountains would disappear as noted in Isaiah 40, every valley would be filled and every mountain and hill brought low. As noted, before, Habakkuk poetically writes of this event:

8 Was the LORD displeased against the rivers? was thine anger against the rivers? was thy wrath against the sea, that thou didst ride upon thine horses and thy chariots of salvation?

*9 Thy bow was made quite naked, **according to the oaths of the tribes**, even thy word. Selah. **Thou didst cleave the earth with rivers.***

*10 The **mountains saw thee, and they trembled:** the overflowing of the water passed by: **the deep uttered his voice, and lifted up his hands on high.***

*11 The **sun and moon stood still in their habitation: at the light of thine arrows they went, and at the shining of thy glittering spear.***

*12 Thou **didst march through the land in indignation, thou didst thresh the heathen in anger.***

In verse 10 above the deep, the abyss, is raised to form the new heaven, doubtless; the sun and moon are said to stand still in consternation, as they would appear to do as the tectonic plates went back to their earlier positions. In effect, to one standing in England the Eurasian plates, of which Europe is a part, would move westward, towards the mid Atlantic ridge, thus the time would change with regard to the sun. Similarly with the American plates, which would move eastward. This probable interpretation is not stated as such in the Bible, but would accord with the sun and moon standing still.

The language of the prophet coincides and is reminiscent of that of Joel (3:12-17; 2:10-11, 30-31). **Joel 2:9-11 (KJV)**

9 They shall run to and fro in the city; they shall run upon the wall, they shall climb up upon the houses; they shall enter in at the windows like a thief.

The earth shall quake before them; the heavens shall tremble: the sun and the moon shall be dark, and the stars shall withdraw their shining:

*10 **And the LORD shall utter his voice before his army: for his camp is very great: for he is strong that executeth his word: for the day of the LORD is great and very terrible; and who can abide it?***

The expression above in Habakkuk 3:9, the ***oaths of the tribes*** is noted as the word of God.

13 *Thou wentest forth for the salvation of thy people, even for salvation with thine anointed; thou woundedst the head out of the house of the wicked, by discovering the foundation unto the neck. Selah.*

14 *Thou didst strike through with his staves the head of his villages: they came out as a whirlwind to scatter me: their rejoicing was as to devour the poor secretly.*

15 *Thou didst walk through the sea with thine horses, through the heap of great waters.*

16 *When I heard, my belly trembled; my lips quivered at the voice: rottenness entered into my bones, and I trembled in myself, that I might rest in the day of trouble: when he cometh up unto the people,*

he will invade them with his troops.

17 *Although the fig tree shall not blossom, neither shall fruit be in the vines; the labour of the olive shall fail, and the fields shall yield no meat; the flock shall be cut off from the fold, and there shall be no herd in the stalls:*

18 *Yet I will rejoice in the LORD, I will joy in the God of my salvation.*

19 *The LORD God is my strength, and he will make my feet like hinds' feet, and he will make me to walk upon my high places. To the chief singer on my stringed instruments.*

In summary, this momentous event is described in Zechariah 13:6 to 14:9, in what may be called the Coronation of the Lord as the nation of Israel ask of the wounds in His hands and Christ calls them My people and they call him My God. In chapter 14, the Coming of Christ in unimaginable glory, splendour and power; His feet touching Mt. Olivet and the city splitting and moving northward and southward to give place to living waters flowing from Jerusalem, begin His millennial reign on His throne of glory.

In Isaiah 34; in Habakkuk 3; in 2 Peter 3; in Matthew 24:27-42; in 2 Thessalonians 1:7-2:8; indeed, throughout the writings of the Apostle Paul, the Coming of Christ in fire and great glory and power is clearly described and foretold.

The esteemed writer of "*Things to come,*" has influenced the majority of Evangelicals in misreading 2 Peter chapter 3. He quotes the King James translation of verse 7 of this portion, which, as noted previously speaks of the day of judgment and perdition of ungodly men, instead of *a* day of judgment and perdition of (living) ungodly men, as noted In Acts 17:31 and Jude. This is not the judgment of the Great white throne, where it is the *dead* that stand before Christ.

CHAPTER 11

CURRENT EVENTS & PROPHECY

Focusing on Prophecy brings the present realities into a direct line of vision as to where the world is heading and how remarkable well events fit together culminating in their fulfillment. Many are vitally concerned with events of the last year, the earthquakes, fires, storms, floods, tornadoes, pandemics and other unusual occurrences as well as the unsettled actions, threats, and dispositions of the nations on earth.

To His disciple's questions about the end of the age, Christ recalled the times of Noah's Flood; the judgment of Sodom and Gomorrah; and such devastating conditions to come that unless the days were shortened, no flesh would be saved. However, for the elect's sake mankind would be saved. It should be borne in mind that God has a definite plan and purpose to save as many as will come to Him in repentance and faith. What happens between now and the end time is the subject of this chapter. The Apostle Paul warns his co-worker Timothy that, "2 Timothy 3:1-7 (KJV)

1 This knows also, that in the last days perilous times shall come.

2 For men shall be lovers of their own selves, covetous, boasters, proud, blasphemers, disobedient to parents, unthankful, unholy,

3 Without natural affection, trucebreakers, false accusers, incontinent, fierce, despisers of those that are good,

4 Traitors, heady, high-minded, lovers of pleasures more than lovers of God;

5 Having a form of godliness, but denying the power thereof: from such turn away.

6 For of this sort are they which creep into houses, and lead captive silly women laden with sins, led away with diver's lusts,

7 Ever learning, and never able to come to the knowledge of the truth."

This is a severe list of offences and behaviour that merits judgment. It is emblematic of a severe degradation from the standards of life taught and lived by the Apostle. The end of the age will come too with a falling away from Biblical standards and practices into apostasy from the Faith and adherence to the Gospel of Christ. During nearly the last century, the writer has noticed this falling away from the time of President Dwight Eisenhower's introduction of the teaching of Evolution into the schools and colleges, followed by the consequential throwing out of the Bible even in the law courts and the market place. The degenerate life and practices of the general public from the sexual revolution of the 1960's to the confusion of the sexes today, only follows the expected pattern leading to divine intervention to save mankind from itself. As the prophecies of the Bible unfold, such as the reconstitution of Israel into the land; the line-up and amalgamation of nations into that prophesied; there can be no doubt that we are the terminal 'generation that will not have passed away till all things are fulfilled.'

The next great climactic, revolutionary development is the Rapture or snatching away of the church, just preceding the appearance and revelation of the Anti-Christ, the man of sin. In 1 Thessalonians 4:13-18 (KJV)

13 But I would not have you to be ignorant, brethren, concerning them which are asleep, that ye sorrow not, even as others which have no hope.

14 For if we believe that Jesus died and rose again, even so them also which sleep in Jesus will God bring with him.

15 For this we say unto you by the word of the Lord, that we which are alive and remain unto the coming of the Lord shall not prevent them which are asleep.

16 For the Lord himself shall descend from heaven with a shout, with

the voice of the archangel, and with the trump of God: and the dead in Christ shall rise first:

17 Then we which are alive and remain shall be caught up together with them in the clouds, to meet the Lord in the air: and so, shall we ever be with the Lord.

18 Wherefore comfort one another with these words.

This portion is contiguous with that in:

1 Corinthians 15:51-55 (KJV)

51Behold, I shew you a mystery; We shall not all sleep, but we shall

all be changed,

52In a moment, in the twinkling of an eye, at the last trump: for the trumpet shall sound, and the dead shall be raised incorruptible, and we shall be changed.

53For this corruptible must put on in corruption, and this mortal must put on immortality.

54So when this corruptible shall have put on in corruption, and this mortal shall have put on immortality, then shall be brought to pass the saying that is written, Death is swallowed up in victory.

55O death, where is thy sting? O grave, where is thy victory?

It is to be noted that this coming of the Lord to snatch away His church is done unexpectedly, in the blink of an eyes, all the saints are caught up to meet Christ in the clouds of heaven and return to heaven, thus fulfilling the promise of Christ that if I go away, I'll come again and receive you unto Myself, that where I am ye may be also. (John 14:1). After seven years of the Great Tribulation takes place, Christ returns to earth with all His saints and myriads of His Holy Angels to execute judgment of fire on the earth and set up a new world wherein dwells righteousness, ending as noted in this book.

As the Apostle wrote, (2 Corinthians 6:1-2):

"We then...beseech you also, that ye receive not the grace of God in vain. (For He saith, I have heard the in a time accepted, and in the day of salvation have I succoured thee: behold now is the accepted time: behold now is the day of Salvation.)" Close in with the Divine offer.

The Prophetic future, the current circumstances, and developments on earth can only really be understood by going back to the very beginning of creation, viewing the major developments, judgments and interventions of God in human affairs, to comprehend the end of all things.

All things and peoples were created for the pleasure and by the will of the Creator, a God of love, holiness, and grace. Love can only be found and exercised in an atmosphere of free will. Free will entails the choice and possibility of rebellion against these standards. The bible explains that Lucifer, the Light-bearer, was created perfect in all his ways, with beauty, knowledge and understanding, perfect. Because of these attributes pride filled his heart and mind, bringing upon him and the third of the angels with him, a downfall that ends in the judgment of eternal hell of fire. The rescue of mankind who fell at his temptation, embraces the whole bible.

This rescue entails the curse on man and earth, all to bring back man to a true and sincere and obedient state. Two peoples are then formed, those who bow, accept, obey, and love the Creator and those who side with Lucifer, now known as Satan, the opposer of God and all that is good, holy and true. Hardship, sorrow, grief. adversity and death are the necessary results of sin and disobedience. Had edenic conditions continued after the Fall of man, all would have led to further corruption; very few rich and prosperous people find or obey the straight and narrow way that leads to godly sorrow and repentance, a reception of the only provided Saviour and Lord Jesus Christ. Broad is the road, and wide is the way that leads to destruction, and many there are who go into it. The intervention of the judgment of the Great world-wide Flood of Noah's day, was to save humanity from its own corruption. The destruction of Sodom and Gomorrah; the plagues of Egypt; the deliverance of Israel; the giving of the Ten commandments, were all to teach wayward mankind the ways of God and form a chosen nation through whom the divine Saviour would come, die, redeem, and pay the penalty of man's sins so God could justly be reconciled to sinful man, change him and grant eternal life and pardon to him. Through His resurrection and Ascension, the Holy Spirit of God Himself can now indwell man, have fellowship with him and enjoy and experience the love and grace of a truly good, holy, and only God, Creator of heaven and earth and all therein.

On the other hand, all those who reject God's loving, pardoning offer, must, with Satan, his angels and rebels suffer eternal, burning punishment away from the very loving Presence, grace, and love of God and his holy angels.

The prophetic word therefore relates the coming return of Christ for His saints; the rise and world-wide exercise of power of the man of sin, known as Antichrist, the beast. Seven years of Tribulation then follow in which God judges the earth and the world. Those who accept the final message and repent, refusing this despot, pay with their lives and join the redeemed after the glorious return of Christ in flaming fire and judgment to set up his eternal kingdom and the Palingenesis of the heaven and earth.

ADDENDA

PALESTINE, ARABS & ISLAMIC ALLIES

The writer wishes to add this fulfillment of a chapter found in his previous book (printed in 2014), called *"Portentous End Time Prophecies"*, as it reflects how quickly events happen and change. The IVth chapter, entitled *Palestine, Arabs & Islamic Allies*, shows how, in just 8 short years these changes have come to pass. Here it is:

The Philistines, dwelling along the coast around Gaza, were called Cherethites, thus again reinforcing the fact that they came from Crete.

The origin of the name Palestine may not be too well known to many in the English-speaking world, but it is quite evident in the Hebrew. The word Philistine is readily recognized in the Hebrew word **פלשתים** – pelishtim-; as well as in the word **כרתים** -ceretim-(plural of crt=crete) found in **Zephaniah 2:5 (Hebrew Bible)**

5 :הוי ישבי חבל הים גוי כרתים דבר־יהוה עליכם כנען ארץ פלשתים והאבדתיך מאין יושב ה

This is called the land of the Philistines above. The initial letter is sounded as the English P or F, (ph). In Spanish it is *Filisteo*. It means "the land of wanderers; strangers" being undoubtedly a reference to the origin of these people who came as *"refugees"* and were "strangers or foreigners" fleeing the great volcanic disaster in Crete about 1500 B.C. This too, is corroborated in the name given them in the Septuagint Greek version, translated in the third century B.C. In this version they are called Αλλοφυλοι (allophuloi), *the other tribe,* from the Greek αλλος (allos), *other, and* φυλη (phule), *tribe.*

They are referred to as the *nation of the Cherethites,* in the same verse above. The Hebrew consonants Ch, r, and t, are clearly seen and the word would correspond to the English name Crete.

The Philistines came to the coasts of Palestine about 1500 B.C. This was after the great volcanic explosion at Thera, also called Santorini, some 70 miles north-east of Crete. In Jeremiah 47:4b, this origin is clearly stated: *"For the Lord will spoil* **the Philistines, the remnant** *of the country of Caphtor."* Captor is the old name for Crete, and the *remnant,* Hebrew שארית (Shearit), signifies *"survivors, remaining part."* **Jeremiah 47:4 (Hebrew Bible)**

4 כי־שדד יהוה את־**פלשתים שארית אי כפתור**:

Writing in the National Geographic book, *Greece and Rome, builders of our world,* Emily Vermeule notes:

One day near the year 1500 B.C., a tremendous, almost unimaginable explosion shook the Mediterranean world. Boulders the size of houses shot far into the air. Showers of lava, cooled to pumice, rained down on land and sea. The sea bed shuddered and the shock ran along the fault which cleaves the underwater crust between Turkey and Sicily. The volcanic island of Thera was erupting. The erup-tion had heaped 30 to 120 feet of this debris over the Bronze Age surface of the island. This catastrophe resulted in the transfer of a people and their advanced Minoan civilization to the shores of Palestine. The prophet Amos also gave the origin of the Philistines as from Caphtor (Crete), saying:

Amos 9:7 (KJV)

7Have not I brought up Israel out of the land of Egypt? and the Philistines from Caphtor, and the Syrians from Kir?

The explosion on Thera, just seventy miles from Crete would have brought tidal waves one hundred and sixty feet high over its coast. Thera lies at the southern part of the circle of the islands called the Cyclades and the volcano is still active. The Hebrew form of Caphtor (כפתור) signifies "*crown, circlet; Caphtor."* The Greek cyclops, -κυκλωψ– means "*Round-eye*"; and κυκλος, (cyclos) is *a ring, round, circle.* The name of these islands, therefore, seems to characterize their circular form, culminating in the island of Crete itself. It seems likely that Caphtor refers to the entire circle of islands, and Crete primarily to the island known as Crete today. It is a rich land full of all kinds of fruits probably due to its volcanic soil.

It is not surprising, therefore, that one of their own writers said *"the Cretans are...evil beasts, slow bellies" (Titus I:12).* In the Bible the Philistines are described as having advanced weapons for that time. The Israelites themselves, could not drive out these peoples because they had chariots of iron and a more advanced mechanized culture. In 1899 the British archeologist Arthur Evans discovered at Knossos in Crete, an ancient civilization which he named Minoan, because the bull was worshipped there and the fabled minotaurs (Greek -μινος -minus, the name of the *king* and ταυρος-tauros, *bull*) were located there. These minotaurs were said to be half bull, half man, dwelling in the labyrinth of Crete. These elaborate labyrinths contained remarkable frescos. Some 35 years later the Greek archeologist, Speridon Marinatos discovered in Crete the evidence of *a cataclysmic volcanic eruption on Santorini about 1500 B.C. equivalent to 150 hydrogen bombs, the centre of Santorini ripped open as 50 cubic miles of rock vaporized, debris was hurled as far afield as Egypt and Israel, gigantic tsunamis overwhelmed coastlines everywhere in the Mediterranean and aftershocks were felt all over the world. The island of Santorini was shattered into fragments of its former self.*

At Akritaria (Akrotiri) was found a city *entombed by a 30-foot layer of volcanic pumice for more than 3 ½ thousand years, the city was clearly related to the ruins of Minoan Crete...among the city's ruins was evidence of a complex drainage system, showers, flushing toilets, even hot and cold running water. Here too were exquisite wall paintings, their rich colours preserved by the centuries of confinement...*

The chief cities of the Philistines were known as Gaza, Askelon, Ashdod, and Ekron. They inhabited the sea coast around these towns and were also referred to as the Cherethites. This Hebrew word כרתים (Cheretim), forms the base of the Greek word Κρητη (Krete, Crete), which corresponds to the English Crete. In the Bible, the Philistines, dwelling along the coast around Gaza, were called Cherethites, thus again reinforcing the fact that they came from Crete. In the German Bible this verse is also clearly identified:

Wehe den Bewohnern des Landstrichs am Meer, der Nation der Kreter; a footnote adds: "Gemeint sind die Philister." This means "commonly called the Philistines"; referring to "the nation of Crete, (Cretans)."

In the prophecy of Zephaniah (1:14-18), the time referred to is that of *the great day of the Lord, the day of the Lord's wrath and judgment,* at the time of the appearance of Christ on Mt. Olivet, as previously noted. Great destructions and devastations are foretold upon those dwelling in this region of Palestine where the Philistines once dwelt. It may be questioned why this information about these people is relevant in the context of Scripture or this book, but it is evident that it is another instance of God bringing judgment on a people who had transgressed beyond the pale, having perverted their ways in dissolute living and deviant practices.

Divine judgment fell upon Crete at Santorini, in the form of this violent volcanic eruption affecting the entire Mediterranean basin. This is likewise comparable to the destruction of Sodom and Gomorrah some 600-700 years earlier whose deviant practices, shameless living, fullness of bread, and abundant idleness brought on their destruction with fire and brimstone from heaven obliterating the entire area. This was set forth as an example to those that would live ungodly and walk after the evil imaginations of the heart. Again, in the eruption of Mount Vesuvius and the destruction of the city of Pompeii in Italy, their evil deeds are recorded in the recent uncovering of the site. So, debase were the drawings on the walls that they were covered up by the authorities from the visiting tourists. The destruction by the worldwide flood of Noah's day was due to the fact that every imagination of the thoughts of the hearts of the people of that day was evil continually. Christ prophesied that as it was in the days of Noah, so shall it be before the Coming of the Son of man. In Noah's day it is written that the very angels of heaven saw the beauty of daughters of men and took them wives, as many as they chose. To this union was born giants who became men of renown.

Genesis 6:1-5 (KJV)

1 And it came to pass, when men began to multiply on the face of the earth, and daughters were born unto them,

*2 That the **sons of God saw the daughters of men** that they were fair; and they took them wives of all which they chose.*

3 And the LORD said, my spirit shall not always strive with man, for that he also is flesh: yet his days shall be an hundred and twenty years.

4 There were giants in the earth in those days; and also, after that, when the sons of God came in unto the daughters of men, and they bare children to them, the same became mighty men which were of old, men of renown.

5 And GOD saw that the wickedness of man was great in the earth, and that every imagination of the thoughts of his heart was only evil continually.

The Hebrew original called these angels Nephalim from the Hebrew הנפלים (hanefelim) meaning *the fallen ones.*

Genesis 6:2-4 (Hebrew Bible)

2 ב אשר מכל נשים להם ויקחו הנה טבת כי האדם בנות את-בנות **בני-האלהים** ויראו
בחרו:

3 ג ועשרים מאה ימיו והיו בשר הוא בשגם לעלם באדם רוחי לא-ידון יהוה ויאמר
שנה:

4 ד בנות -אל האלהים בני יבאו אשר אחרי-כן וגם ההם בימים בארץ היו **הנפלים**
השם: אנשי מעולם הגברים המה להם וילדו האדם

No doubt the Greek myths and stories of the gods and women stem from true realities both before and after the Flood. The story of the giant Goliath, another example perhaps of angels and women living together, emphasizes the nature and times of the Philistines, the refugees who came from Crete, having an advanced civilization. They had chariots of iron which prevented the Israelites from driving them out of the land.

They even had to go to them to sharpen their tools. It should not be surprising that in our current days of advanced discoveries and development in knowledge and sciences, that man would find more leisure time and opportunities to follow the desires of his own heart and corrupt himself and his very civilization! History repeats itself. It is this very worldwide corruption and inventions that will bring on the just and holy judgment of God against deviant human behaviour.

In as much as this work treats largely of judgment and the coming divine catastrophic events even more terrible than the Flood of Noah, it must be remembered that God is the Person who is most grieved over the necessity of destroying so much of mankind. He is not willing that any should perish but that all should come to repentance and faith in the Lord Jesus. In the matter of the flood it is written:

Genesis 6:4-7 (KJV)

4 There were giants in the earth in those days; and also after that, when the sons of God came in unto the daughters of men, and they bare children to them, the same became mighty men which were of old, men of renown.

5 And GOD saw that the wickedness of man was great in the earth, and that every imagination of the thoughts of his heart was only evil continually.

*6 And it repented the LORD that he had made man on the earth, and **it grieved him at his heart.***

7 And the LORD said, I will destroy man whom I have created from the face of the earth; both man, and beast, and the creeping thing, and the fowls of the air; for it repenteth me that I have made them.

It becomes necessary to destroy mankind to save him from his own destruction. This has ever been the purpose of God in bringing judgment upon man. Even if only a remnant is saved, it becomes the will and purpose of God to deliver man from his own waywardness and create a pure and holy generation of people. In the prophecy of Zephaniah (1:14-18), the time referred to is that of *the great day of the Lord, the day of the Lord's wrath*, at the time of the appearance of Christ on Mt. Olivet, as previously noted. Great destruction and devastation are foretold upon those dwelling in this region of Palestine where the Philistines once dwelt. It is also noteworthy that in the same portion of Zephaniah where these towns of the Philistines are mentioned (Chapter 2:4,5), the context immediately focuses on the children of Ammon and Moab, who are the present day occupants of the land there. Amman in Jordan, is equivalent in Hebrew or Arabic to Ammon, from whom the Ammonites are descended. The Jordanians, therefore, can be called the modern Ammonites, whose capital city Ammon spans thousands of years. Together with the Moabites, also the descendants of Lot, (the father of both Ammon and Moab), parts of the land of Palestine, Jordan, and Saudi Arabia are being occupied by them today. Calling themselves Palestinians, these groups of people, together with other Arab immigrants from neighbouring countries, now claim the land of Israel. Zephaniah delineates how they have reproached and reviled Israel, claiming their rights to the land.

*8 I have heard **the reproach** of Moab, and the **revilings of the children of Ammon**, whereby **they have reproached my people, and magnified themselves against their border.***

9 Therefore as I live, saith the LORD of hosts, the God of Israel, Surely Moab shall be as Sodom, and the children of Ammon as Gomorrah, even the breeding of nettles, and saltpits, and a perpetual desolation: the residue of my people shall spoil them, and the remnant of my people shall possess them.

*10 This shall they have for their pride, **because they have reproached and magnified themselves against the people of the LORD of hosts.***

11 The LORD will be terrible unto them: for he will famish all the gods of the earth; and men shall worship him, every one from his place, even all the isles of the heathen. **Zephaniah 2:8-11 (KJV)**

The land of Palestine was chosen of God to be the place where He would place His name as a witness to all the world of His goodness, mercy, and salvation of the entire human race. Israel was placed there with His temple in the midst of them in Jerusalem. The nation was warned that they would be scattered abroad the whole world should they disobey and practice evil and serve the gods of the nations. There was however, a promise that *they would be brought back at the end time* and be reconciled to God after great judgments and tribulations on the earth. This is the time in which they are now found. The Arab nations have occupied the land of Israel for nearly 2,000 years since the rulers and people of Israel rejected the promised Messiah, in Jesus Christ of Nazareth. God has not been oblivious to the world in the last 2,000 years but has sent the promise and message of Salvation to every nation and tongue under heaven. In accordance with the promises and prophecies of the Bible, He is *now regathering the nation of Israel into the land.* The Arab nations in it and surrounding it are all against this divine plan and eternal purpose of God. As noted above they have *magnified themselves against my boarders, and reproached his people, Israel.*

The nations of the world have divided the land and are in effect trying to short-circuit the divine plans and purposes. This therefore brings all the nations into antagonism with God. This will lead to the gathering of the nations at Armageddon and the eventual return of Christ to save and deliver His people Israel.

The Islamic nations surrounding Israel are ever determined to frustrate this plan of God, substituting instead the teachings of their religion and putting their founder, Mohamed above the teachings of the Bible and the Lord's Christ. The Psalmist declared in the Biblical prophecies that this would be the case.

Psalm 83:1-18 (KJV)

[1] *Keep not thou silence, O God: hold not thy peace, and be not still, O God.*

[2] *For, lo, thine enemies make a tumult:* **and they that hate thee have lifted up the head.**

[3] *They have taken crafty counsel against thy people, and consulted against thy hidden ones.*

[4] **They have said, Come, and let us cut them off from being a nation; that the name of Israel may be no more in remembrance.**

[5] **For they have consulted together** *with one* **consent:** *they are confederate against thee:*

[6] *The tabernacles of* **Edom, and the Ishmaelites; of Moab, and the Ha- garenes;**

[7] **Gebal, and Ammon, and Amalek; the Philistines with the inhabitants of Tyre;**

[8] **Assur also is joined with them: they have holpen the children of Lot.** *Selah.*

[9] *Do unto them as unto the Midianites; as to Sisera, as to Jabin, at the brook of Kison:*

[10] *Which perished at Endor: they became as dung for the earth.*

[11] *Make their nobles like Oreb, and like Zeeb: yea, all their princes as Zebah, and as Zalmunna:*

[12] *Who said, Let us take to ourselves* **the houses of God in possession.**

[13] *O my God, make them like a wheel; as the stubble before the wind.*

14 As the fire burneth a wood, and as the flame setteth the mountains on fire;

15 So persecute them with thy tempest, and make them afraid with thy storm.

16 Fill their faces with shame; that they may seek thy name, O LORD.

17 Let them be confounded and troubled forever; yea, let them be put to shame, and perish:

18 That men may know that thou, whose name alone is JEHOVAH, art the most high over all the earth.

The nations mentioned in this passage, including Assur (Iraq), and Saudi Arabia and the descendants of Hagar, called here the Hagarenes, all join forces and purposes to destroy Israel completely and cause them to cease from being a nation. Added to this group is the Islamic nation of Iran who have publicly called for the wiping off the map of Israel. The previous Prime Minister loudly proclaimed that they are expecting their ruler the Mahdi to come and rule the earth and destroy Israel. The intention of Islam is to rule the whole earth. It may well be that he is the one spoken of in the Scriptures who will exalt himself and rule the world during the seven-year Tribulation period. All who proclaim Christ will be put to death. This is being done even today in some of these Islamic nations, when any convert to Christianity. We may be closer than we think to the end time when ominous, catastrophic and cosmic events are about to come to pass on the whole earth.

www.ingramcontent.com/pod-product-compliance
Lightning Source LLC
Chambersburg PA
CBHW051008140626
46546CB00016B/1305